Dream Catcher 47

Stairwell Books //

Dream Catcher 47

SUBSCRIPTIONS TO
DREAM CATCHER
MAGAZINE

£15.00 UK (Two issues inc. p&p)
£22.00 Europe
£25.00 USA and Canada

Cheques should be made
payable to **Dream Catcher**
and sent to:

Dream Catcher Subscriptions
161 Lowther Street
York, YO31 7LZ
UK

+44 1904 733767

argillott@gmail.com

www.dreamcatchermagazine.co.uk
@literaryartsmag
www.stairwellbooks.co.uk
@stairwellbooks

Dream Catcher Magazine

Dream Catcher No. 47

The moral rights of authors and artists have been asserted

ISSN: 1466-9455

Published by Stairwell Books //

ISBN: 978-1-913432-76-8

York UNESCO
City of Media Arts

Contents – Authors

Featured Artist *Chantal Barnes*   1
Editorial *Hannah Stone*   3
Obituary for Clint Wastling *Hannah Stone*   4
Tractor *Harry Slater*   6
High Tea *Chris Scriven*   7
Worm of Discontent *Bill Fitzsimons*   8
Temporary Husband *Steven Sivell*   9
Holiday Romance *George Jowett*   10
The One Who Stayed Home *Owen O'Sullivan*   12
Quickly Wood *Paul Brownsey*   13
Son House and the Mock Tortoiseshell Beatle Boots *David Danbury* 19
Introduction and Allegro *Clifford Liles*   20
Moonlight *Knotbrook Taylor*   21
Honeyman *Sue Moules*   22
Uffern Gwaedlyd *Michael W Thomas*   23
A Memorable Lesson *Wilf Deckner*   24
Stray *David McVey*   26
Did You Have a Good War? *Steven Sivell*   31
Mohini *Jaspreet Mander*   32
Writing on Air Fest 2022 *Jaimes Lewis Moran*   36
The Writing Poetry Poem *Knotbrook Taylor*   39
The Whole is Greater Than the Some of Its Poets *Simon Tindale*   40
Farewell *Paula Jennings*   41
Before Hiroshima, Before Nagasaki – There Was Trinity *Mark Pearce*   42
Night-Time Economy *Jane Ayrie*   44
Scales Grade 1 – 8 and Beyond *Jane Sharp*   50
Music in the Raw *Michael Newman*   51
Is Blue an Illusion? *Lauren K. Nixon*   52
The Clouds *Joseph Estevez*   53
A Near-Drowning and a Lightning Rescue *Philip Burton*   54
The Field *Ray Malone*   55
Devizes White Horse *Jeff Phelps*   56
Velvet Underpants *Lauren K. Nixon*   57

Prayer Flags of the Oppressed *D M Street*   58

Such Tales They Had to Tell *Denise McSheehy*   60

Mirror Agreement *Michael Penny*   63

Lairage *Edward Alport*   64

Northumbrian Piper *Dave Medd*   65

August *Michael W Thomas*   66

Harvest Combinations *Rob Peel*   67

The Inevitable *Niels Hammer*   69

The Dialect of Winter *Michael Henry*   71

Frozen *Andria Cooke*   72

The Ministry of Fear *Michael Henry*   73

How *Not* to See Ourselves as Ithers See Us *Bob Cooper*   74

Selfie *Graham Mort*   75

Rose Garden *Graham Mort*   76

Since Her Stroke, She Mourns *John Michael Sears*   77

The Marchioness at the Edge of Clifton Suspension Bridge *Kathryn Moores*   78

Stoic *Liz McPherson*   79

No Body *Tonnie Richmond*   80

Forensic *Dave Medd*   82

Golem *Andy Humphrey*   83

Mer-Man *Andy Humphrey*   84

Alcuin *Colin Speakman*   85

Pain Pathway *Laura Strickland*   86

Taking Flight *James B. Nicola*   87

The Unravelling *Laura Strickland*   88

Change and No Change *Bob Cooper*   89

Decommissioned Police Car *Steven Sivell*   90

The Nice Man *Adam Strickson*   91

Witnessing *Heather Deckner*   93

How to Get Back into Your Body *Emily Zobel Marshall*   94

The Slow Slipping Drift of It *Steven Lightfoot*   95

There Wasn't Much Left, in All Honesty *Miles Salter*   97

The Lookout *David Thompson*   98

How You Rose *Emily Zobel Marshall*   99

Peanut *Verity Baldry*   100

No One Tells You *Laura Strickland*   101

Miscarriage *Dave Medd*   102

It's for the Best *Sandra Noel*   103

Reviews   104

Imperfect Beginnings by Viv Fogel *Patrick Lodge*   104

Flamingo by Kathryn Bevis *Hannah Stone*   106

The Way Taken: A Chinese Expedition by Dave Wynne-Jones
Pauline Kirk   107

Bodies and other haunted houses by S L Grange *Hannah Stone*   108

Something the Colour of Pines on Fire by Vahid Davar *Patrick Lodge*   109

Surrender by Cathy Grindrod *Nick Allen*   111

Journey Into Space by Seán Street *Hannah Stone*   112

Angola, America by Sammy Weaver *Nick Allen*   113

The Doll's Hospital by Jenny Robb *Hannah Stone*   115

Index of Authors   117

FEATURED ARTIST
ARTIST STATEMENT: CHANTAL BARNES

There is a misconception that Abstract Painting in its composition floats free of concrete representation. Subject matter? Colour scheme? Mark making? Throw them up in the air, the presumption goes, and let them land where they may. Since the Industrial Revolution, Freud, and Photography, when populations boomed and the subconscious floated up as a dominant conduit, Modern Art has been almost obliged to interpret the world in whatever way the artist wants.

This has naturally extended to Poetry. e.e. cummings, one of the 20th century's leading poets, gives us anyone lived in a pretty how town, where the title of the poem is its first line and provides us with an aesthetically pleasing enigma. Emily Dickinson's 'The brain is wider than the sky' is instantly absurd. The physical brain is not wider than the sky, nor, as she asserts later, is it 'deeper than the sea'. Her play with concepts, however, the physicality of the brain and the abstract notion of the mind, provides a timely portal in our discussion of this issue's painter, Chantal Barnes.

Barnes' paintings are based on the building blocks of concrete representation. Her seascapes have languid tides and her landscapes have foregrounds and iridescent horizons. They are also shot through with elements of Abstract Art. In her hands, skies pullulate and colours throb as if seen for the first time. For Contemporary Painters, few inspirational visual touchstones inculcate the mixing of colours and the making of marks than the relentless crests of breaking waves, and it is this, in her latest collection, Chantal Barnes concurs with Emily Dickinson. The mind is indeed wider than the sky and deeper than the sea: it is the mind which can endow, through personal Abstract flourishes, new ways of looking at that which we may have been taking for granted for too long. Nature not only heals, it galvanises. At a time when we have been fragmented, made afraid, and even a walk on a beach has been coldly enumerated (drone footage of lone dog walkers on beaches being castigated by tannoys brings back bad memories), the horizon, and its promise of light amidst elemental darkness, is perhaps the crucial message Chantal Barnes in her paintings imparts.

Greg McGee

PAGES OF ARTWORK

Infinite	*Cover*
Infinite II	11
Infinite III	25
Reflections of Clouds	38
Sun Drenched Reflection	49
We Met When We Were Almost Young	59
Throwback	70
Cocoon	81
Just Behind the Morning	92

Welcome to DC 47 and a jam-packed issue of stories, poems, memoirs and reviews.

After the political and emotional storms of 2022, it feels almost as if summer 2023 is in the doldrums. We haven't had a new prime minister or monarch for *ages*, nor an extreme weather event worth recording (which of course is tempting fate). That big 'do' in London has been and gone without major incident, Leeds United has been relegated, and no-mow May has yielded a somewhat underwhelming range of offerings for pollinators this year (have to get a sustainability mention in, to sustain our eco-credentials).

From out the still, misty waters of spring 2023 emerge, Nessie-like (or channelling Excalibur?), visions, ghosts, subconscious desires and fears in the form of Mermen, close encounters with Thor, holocaust survivors, bathers cursing in Welsh, new planets in the making. We meet a nameless (but adored) farm vehicle, dodge stray bombs, excavate human remains, say farewells, consume the world, avoid Jehovah's Witnesses, and learn how to get back into our bodies. We celebrate bagpipes and velvet underpants. We have an unusual number of villanelles. We have reflections on the process of writing (and performing). In the rich medley of offerings I am, as always, touched by the creativity, honesty, tenderness, rage, despair, and joy which you writers pin down on the page for us to read. We love fostering the community which is Dream Catcher.

On a more sombre note, the editorial/publishing crew were stopped in our tracks by the passing of one of our number. We honour Clint Wastling, and dedicate this edition of Dream Catcher to his memory. Reflections from the editorial team may be found below.

We're open for submissions for DC 48, and the website has been updated, courtesy of Stairwell, so do head over to that if you're planning to ask us to read your work, so you know what to do and what to expect. It's always a pleasure, as a team, to engage in this process and we are delighted to welcome Will Kemp, a poet and short story writer especially well known to York folk, and also further afield, to the panel of 'readers' of your submissions. Keep 'em coming!

Hannah Stone

It was with great sadness that the editorial team learned, in February, of the death at the age of 63 of Clint Wastling, a valued member of the 'reading team' of Dream Catcher submissions, and himself a published author of poetry, novels, short stories and plays. He created a literary page in the 'Just Beverley' journal, and his practice was embedded in the landscape and prehistory of East Yorkshire, as well as the emotional and psychological geographies of LGBTQ+ and fantasy. Clint received a terminal diagnosis in the autumn of 2022, and with his customary modesty did not want attention drawn to his condition. Stairwell Books was delighted to be able to publish his final collection of poetry, *Quiet Flows the Hull*, last year, a companion piece to *Tyrants Rex* (2017) and *Geology of Desire* (2015).

His pamphlet *Layers* was published by Marsden-based Maytree Press, and fellow Maytree poets Joe Williams and Hannah Stone remember fondly the Maytree events Clint organised and participated in, at the Leeds Library and for the Leeds Poetry Festival. He was such an easy person to work with – utterly reliable, always ready to step into the breach (notably for a Leeds Lieder event Hannah was running where at no notice at all he stepped into the breach to provide an additional poet to work with a composer), gracefully contributing as one of a team rather than ever hogging the limelight.

As well as a writer and editor, Clint was a popular teacher (his 'day job' was as a Chemistry teacher) and his ability to empower and support others was striking. Contributions to the local community included a stint as a poet in residence at Burton Constable Hall, and innovative work at his beloved Spurn Point, where the 'layers' of natural history and geology really spoke to him.

Rose and Alan reminisced: Clint was a special person. People say that about others all the time – but Clint truly WAS. He would have been beloved by students: he was beloved by the poetry and sci-fi/fantasy community. Clint was kind, generous, patient and oh so clever.

I loved talking with Clint about poetry, stories, LGBTQ rights, and science fiction conventions. Our entire publishing focus changed because of him: Clint asked if we could bring his then-new book, *Tyrants Rex*, to Fantasycon that November. "Fantasy what?" I replied. Fantasycon: the annual event sponsored by the British Fantasy Society, promoting all things fantasy, sci-fi, and horror. We realised that a few of our books were SFF: we always publish quality fiction, but some were, indeed, sci-fi and fantasy. We went, we loved it, and began bringing out more SFF titles. We always have a grand time.

A few years ago, daughter Emily wanted to go, as usual, to Fantasycon, but Alan and I would be away. Clint offered immediately to drive Em to the event! Brenda and Clint took Em as their passenger; ensured she safely reached her hotel room, registered for the con, and got her delegate badge. After the con ended, they escorted Em to a direct train back to York, even gifting her a delicious lunch for the journey! Brenda and Clint had wanted to drive back to York slowly, sightseeing geological marvels and gorgeous waterfalls along the way. I am so happy they took that opportunity to enjoy their beloved pastime of slow travel and sightseeing. We none of us know how long we have.

However long that is, may we all have such a wonderful impact on friends, family and colleagues as Clint.

Pauline Kirk remembers: Clint was a friend as well as a colleague. We both wrote fantasy/speculative fiction novels, and met at Fantasycon as well as at spoken word and Stairwell Books events. I also contributed stories and poems to Clint's literary page in 'Just Beverley'. I admired him as an editor, poet and novelist, and appreciated his encouragement with my own work. I particularly remember his kindness and good company.

The editorial team would like to join in sending our condolences to Brenda and the family, and in honour of Clint's life we would like to dedicate this issue of Dream Catcher to his memory. We miss you, Clint.

Hannah Stone

TRACTOR

She was the first time I heard my dad say fuck
With venom instead of impish glee
A vision in patches of dust and oil, grass stalks and creeping rust
Red like morning-after eyes and congealing ketchup.
Her tyres swollen and faded to rat-fur grey
A cracked map of pressure you could trace with a careful thumb.
She'd only let me push her clutch, stubborn and strong
And sometimes incapable of turning right, like all the best ones are.
Bedecked with a thin cushion on her folding seat,
A length of hose slipped around her gear stick for better purchase,
Gauges mere suggestions of a past when she spoke to anyone who was interested,
Instead of just me.
Her slow, thudding heartbeat, coaxed to life with Quick Start sprays
Becoming a teeth-shuddering roar when the rotovator dropped
And the PTO was wrangled into its half-press gear.
Balanced out with a barrel full of concrete,
Her forks half hydraulic and oozing, half a lever that let gravity do its job.
Rocking and threatening to overturn but never reaching that point of collapse,
Not when I gouged the walls with her flanks,
Or she rolled down that hill going faster than her engine could hope to propel her.
Days spent churning and slicing through the earth
Carving imperfect patterns in the flesh of the world,
With her as my sculptor's tool, my paintbrush, my elephant shit and
formaldehyde.
I never gave her a name, that was something for her to decide,
A secret she kept in the wheeze of her red-hot exhaust
And the refinery stink of her patched up guts.
Even when we got her overhauled, refitted with slicker parts and fresh rubber,
She cooed the softest to my welly meeting the metal of her single step.
My girl never had any brakes, she didn't need them,
Just bricks to rest at when I guided her into the lean-to, warm and dirty and bow-
legged.
I sometimes wonder if she still chugs her way through the mud,
If someone else has fallen for her obstinate charms and lungfuls of smoke
But I'll never go back and check.
She was mine then, and that was enough, perfect and broken and falling to pieces
And I'll wear her diesel stains on my skin forever.

Harry Slater

HIGH TEA

High tea enjoyed unparalleled success
although the late Spring sky was overcast.
I offered you a sandwich, you said 'yes'.

With warmer sun, I might've shaken less,
my hands not trembled as the plates were passed.
High tea enjoyed unparalleled success

No doubt I felt a little under-dressed
when all around exhibited such class.
I offered you a cake and you said 'yes'.

Because I got the table in a mess,
my heart was beating worryingly fast.
High tea enjoyed unparalleled success

Before I suffered cardiac arrest,
I moved towards my final theme at last.
I offered you Prosecco, you said 'yes'.

All secrets have their time to be confessed,
and this one's unimaginably vast.
High tea enjoyed unparalleled success
I offered you a ring and you said 'yes'.

Chris Scriven

I destroyed the only love I ever knew:
she said she loved me and I doubted her –
a worm of discontent inside me grew.

Because I would not trust her to be true
(waiting for betrayal to occur)
I destroyed the only love I ever knew.

Although my reasons were indeed but few
for casting on her name an ugly slur –
a worm of discontent inside me grew.

To control it was more than I could do
and, my fevered mind reacting to the spur,
I destroyed the only love I ever knew.

And, although I tried to build anew
the love we had; to make it stir,
a worm of discontent inside me grew.

Now I know that I will always rue
the pain I let my jealous heart incur:
I destroyed the only love I ever knew –
a worm of discontent inside me grew.

Bill Fitzsimons

All she wants is a temporary husband.
Someone to pick the windblown sheets
from the bramble bushes.
He has a broad back and he's goat-like on the mountain.
But she's had it being mother and father, sister and brother;
he's a born, yet again lover.
Even so, she cannot bear such a long exposure.
She'd rather be walking Greek islands with
parties of strangers who give nothing
and take nothing in return.
Except for the odd wild flower.
Or an ear of roadside corn.
All she wants is someone to hold her.
Someone to let her go.

Steven Sivell

While shrill cicadas serenade our dreams
And cockroaches patrol the dripping shower,
A door slams shut. "You bitch!" A woman screams.

Through the shutters a taxi's headlight beams
Illuminate the lateness of the hour
While shrill cicadas serenade our dreams.

There's romance in the air, and yet it seems
One holiday at least is turning sour.
A door slams shut. "You bitch!" A woman screams.

Across the square each stuttering footstep rhymes
With those, one pace behind, of her pursuer
While shrill cicadas serenade our dreams.

They must have come unstuck, her amorous schemes;
That being so, what can she do but glower?
A door slams shut. "You bitch!" A woman screams.

In mirrored shades, next day, the hot sun gleams;
They hide a bruise, his jealousy's bright flower.
While shrill cicadas serenade our dreams
A door slams shut. "You bitch!" A woman screams.

George Jowett

Re-published, with apologies to George for a previous typo introduced during the editing of DC 46.

Infinite II

I hung the washing out on the line,
To a chorus of morning song
And it was a wonderful feeling for heart and mind,
This early to have something done.

I filled the coal and cleared the grate,
I cleaned the glass stove door
I wiped the surface of every kitchen item,
And then I swept the floor.

I poured the coffee, I buttered toast,
I placed a napkin upon the plate
I took her pills in the palm of my hand,
So their taking would not be late.

I crept in through the bedroom door,
Where she lay within the bed
And as I gave a warm 'Hello',
She coughed like she wished me dead.

Owen O'Sullivan

The condom with its shocking milky content is impaled on a twig of a beech tree. Around the condom, the drab brown autumn leaves have been stripped away to give maximum visibility to the universal affront. As it shudders in the wind under the overcast sky, the last ghosts of Ted's holy dreams vanish from Quickly Wood.

But the flaunted condom would not have befouled Quickly Wood if what Quickly Wood stood for hadn't already been blasted. When Ted and Colin planned their move from the city, the charming name of the wood rising from the edge of the village seemed to promise a narrative of their lives as lives are supposed to be lived. "The walks we took in Quickly Wood," they'd reminisce when they were old. "Remember the time your Mum and Dad got lost in Quickly Wood?" They'd know where the badger setts were, where the toothwort grew. They'd tell friends they must come and see the vistas of bluebells in Quickly Wood. "Yes, an odd name, isn't it? Etymology unknown, apparently. But it's on a hill, the wood, and the hill is sort of cup-shaped, and the Scots for a cup is 'quaich' so could 'Quickly' come from 'quaich'?" Maybe they'd adopt children, for whom their doting dads would arrange Easter egg hunts in Quickly Wood. And if developers or vandals ever threatened Quickly Wood, the fight against them would be led by Ted and Colin, you bet, their manifest love of the wood perhaps even earning them recognition by the locals as the Quickly Wood Boys, cousins of the Folks Who Live On The Hill whom Peggy Lee sang about. Where the trees thinned out, high up, a well-preserved medieval tower-house built by the Earls of Erskine were a promise that Ted and Colin's village happiness in Woodhouse would likewise be mortared into Scotland's history.

But the promise had been worthless, and now Ted wouldn't care if Quickly Wood burnt down. Well, he would. But yesterday, the estate agent hoisted the For Sale sign outside Ted and Colin's house. The lawyer is instructed that the proceeds are to be divided equally between them.

What force had compelled this wee diversion into Quickly Wood when Ted only came out to go to the village shop? Still, perhaps what the used condom did to Quickly Wood is a kindly service, enabling the worst of the pain to be got over faster.

There's no sign of anyone in the shop. The unattended check-out at the entrance speaks of a village haven where you don't need to lock your doors, though in fact there was a robbery with knife threats at the run-down Black Bull Hotel last year. And if a village store conjures thoughts of bread still warm from the baking, milk from the cows in the next field, this one is part of the HandyStore franchise chain, and there's shelf after shelf of fizzy drinks, shelf after shelf of crisps, biscuits, popcorn, factory-made munchies of all kinds in containers up to pillow-case size. Fat chance of the sourdough loaf that Colin, insisting they stick to having meals together despite their occupying different bedrooms, needs for his bread-and-vegetable bake. There'd be fat chance of fresh vegetables, either, but there are enough in the fridge at home after last week's big shop at the Morrisons in Johnstone. A basket at the end of one of the aisles sometimes contains a few potatoes and onions, a cabbage if you're lucky; it's empty today, and the only vegetables ever in the chest display freezer are peas and oven chips. What lives these people live!

No, the shop isn't empty: there's a customer in the post-office alcove at the back. Ted bends in one of the aisles to look for non-scratch scourers. Only abrasive green scourers, unless... He crouches, begins shifting the green scourers to see if there are white non-abrasive ones in behind.

Footsteps tell of Morag returning to the check-out, accompanied by the customer. A female sorrowful voice, vaguely familiar: "And you'll have two less customers soon." Perhaps if he'd thrown himself more into village life he'd have recognised the voice. Were they ever, really, anything but outsiders?

"Oh?" Morag's voice could scratch glass. Long bony face, elaborately made up, hair scraped back.

"The guys in Arran Rise. Colin and the beefy one. Ted. The For Sale sign's gone up at their house."

"They don't do much shopping in here, just bits and pieces."

"Yeah, like I said, everyone driving off to the supermarkets in the towns."

The shelves are tall enough for Ted to walk without being seen from the check-out, but he's crept forward in his crouched position, as if he's in a trench over which bullets are flying, until he glimpses a huge backside in tight black leggings. He jerks back out of possible sight, any noise covered by the hum from the chest freezer. Trish-something, single mother with two or three children. Seems unaware, as she parades through the village with cheery greetings for everyone, of her backside and thighs like a writhing python in a shiny black sack. Big face, voice always eager to mould itself to the other's feelings. Even Ted's, when she greets him, as if she could enter into how he thinks and feels.

He creeps back and repacks the green scourers. No non-abrasive ones.

"Not easy to know. They're all right, though." Morag's voice. "They delivered food orders from here in the lockdown to the old folks in the sheltered housing."

That is NOT buying acceptance. It's just human decency.

"And Colin," Morag continues, "when I got this new cash register, it would just stop working and you had to wait ages till you could ring things up again. He sorted it in five minutes, and wouldn't accept a penny. He's in charge of all the computer stuff for IKEA in Glasgow."

"In charge. That's them. Tell me about it." Trish laughs but it's a very good-natured laugh. "That Litter Patrol thing in Quickly Wood they was in charge of—Ooh, they was slave-drivers. I only went twice. I was sitting having a fag and, well, he didn't say anything, but the beefy one gave me such a look, like I'd crawled out from under. And when we met Jules Hendry with her dog, he told her to pick up the poo, and she was going to anyway, only the dog was still doing it."

Along from the cleaning materials, there are usually some basic medications. Ibuprofen's supposed to be best for muscle pain, of which Ted seems to have suffered a lot since they decided they were through.

"Well, he is a teacher and has to keep the children in order." Morag.

"In Renfrew, isn't it?"

"If you're a teacher, you need to live your life away from the children."

No, only paracetamol, and they've paracetamol at home. Still, he can't go out without buying something, given he's squatting here listening. He lays a packet noiselessly in his basket.

"You don't want the kids looking in the window at you sitting drinking beer in your semmit." Trish laughs again—and is that noise the door opening? "No, they don't either of them have their work here. Who does, though?"

"Who are we talking about?" A man's voice, breathy, wheezy. Is that really cigarette smoke or does the voice alone just conjure up the smell? Charlie Moffat's always hanging around the village, hovering like the Ancient Mariner to talk to people. You're sitting on the Millennium seat at the crossroads, trying to think things through; you smell cigarette smoke, and there's Charlie Moffat materialised next to you, right up close, ratty face, grey hair swept back in a greasy wave; Charlie Moffat starting in about, well, anything at all: the seat itself having been vandalised, the plaster on your finger where you cut yourself opening the tin of tuna, the US President, some passing wee girl's dungarees being far too big for her and, decorated with footballs, obviously her brother's handed down. Sometimes about the big hotel he says he once owned in Crieff, though someone—yes, Cathy Mackinnon, of course—said that's all lies, "like a lot of the things he says". Charlie Moffat, sad loner living alone in some manky room, no domestic life, desperate for company. You could think of him as a village character, Ted supposes.

But thinking of people as village characters is what outsiders do.

"The boys, Colin and Ted," Morag is answering Charlie. "Their house is up for sale."

As silently as a thief, Ted has crept to the far end of the aisle and around into the next aisle. Waddling on his knees, it must look like. Eggs—yes; no free-range, of course. Bread: no sourdough, as he feared; just Kingsmill white sliced. Well, that's what it'll need to be. Acres of cakes in cellophane, many with sickly-looking icing.

"Whether they'll sell it is another thing." Charlie is saying it like someone with a sinister inside story to tell. "No-one's moving to Woodhouse. Bryn and Helen McCue couldn't get the price they needed to buy the house in Troon they put in for. Had to pull out. Trapped here. Rothman's Blue, if you please Morag."

"Nothing to keep them here, though," says Trish. "The boys. Their jobs aren't here. We was just saying."

"That's not why they're moving." The voice goes even lower, luring attention with the promise of dark secrets. "Ructions. Splitting up. At each other's throats."

Are there glances and grimaces, fingers to lips, between the three at the check-out, attempts to communicate or acknowledge Ted's hidden presence? It will only cross his mind some time after he gets home that he might have been visible on CCTV, and by then he won't care.

"Oh dear." Morag.

"Colin poured it all out to me in the Black Bull. Couldn't face going home to the other one when he got off the train." He pauses as though waiting to be egged on.

You just stopped for a drink when you got off the train? Couldn't you let me know? The bloody casserole's dried out!

Eventually, Charlie Moffat continues, "They have to divorce, because they had one of these gay marriages." There's the sound of the door opening again. "So you're losing neighbours, Cathy."

"The two men"—there is a peculiar intonation on the last word—"up the road from me?" That's Cathy Mackinnon. People say they feel sorry for Father Bannon at the Catholic chapel having to put up with Cathy always berating him for introducing innovations into services or not coming down hard enough on moral issues. She stood up and harangued the bishop, too, when he came, for betraying the Catholic faith.

She sighs, as though what's to come is being forced out of her against her will. "Woodhouse won't be any the worse without an example like that for the children. I'm here for a parcel, Morag." Ah, yes, the shop is a pick-up location for stuff ordered online.

There's the sound of a cupboard being unlocked and closed, and Morag says, "Here we are. Mind, they did a lot for the old folk, delivering orders during lockdown."

"Well, fair's fair," Cathy begins, and Ted knows her fair's-fair face, acknowledging that the whole truth has a right to be told but smug that it won't pose the slightest threat to her faith. "They were generous when Bernadette went round the neighbours with our Wee Box for charity."

£20? You're trying to buy acceptance!

Cathy sighs. "But relationships like that, not natural, they can't last."

"Lots of relationships don't last." Morag.

Trish chips in. "Yes, your husband divorced you after only two years, didn't he, Morag?" Was there an emphasis on "divorce" for the sake of someone who doesn't recognise divorce? Not from Trish, surely. She adds, her voice sing-song sympathetic like she knows this makes Morag particularly unhappy, "And it was a Catholic girl, as well, wasn't it?" Charlie Moffat's voice, usually insinuating and a bit whiny, is suddenly assertive. "The boys splitting up, Cathy? Where did you get that idea?"

Keep your voice down. The window's open. Cathy Mackinnon's passing.

"From your own wife, Charlie."

"Then she got hold of the wrong end of the stick. What I told her was, they're moving because there's nothing for them in a dead-and-alive place like Woodhouse. Colin told me one night in the Black Bull."

Ted is still crouched by the bread. Among the cakes adjoining are packs of four iced yum-yums. On an impulse he puts two packs into his basket for himself. Sometimes comfort food is not a substitute for comfort but an enhancer of it.

"That's what I've been saying to Morag. This village drives people away." Trish, her voice so expressive of what she knows Morag wants to express.

And what's that on the shelf beneath the second pack of yum-yums? A £20 note. Because he's crouching, Ted can't quite work it into a front pocket of his cords but slips it into his back pocket. He's stayed concealed from the locals at the check-out for so long that it's now impossible to join them without making clear he's been eavesdropping.

"I always thought," Morag says, "when they were delivering the orders, working together, you could see it, how well they got on together. It was nice."

Opposite the bread and cakes are the ranks of fizzy drinks, giving way to a small section of alcohol. Ted's eyes light on a bottle of Malbec. Colin likes Malbec. To have unburdened himself to Charlie Moffat, he must have been desperate. As Ted lays a bottle in his basket, Trish is saying, "And they organised the clean-up in Quickly Wood. Without them chivvying us we'd never have done it. You need people like them to crack the whip."

There's a brisk "Goodbye" from Cathy and then Trish says she needs to be getting along, too. She adds, "That £20—I wondered if it was stuck to the one I paid you with and, like, showed up extra in the takings."

"It didn't, I'm sorry," says Morag.

"Oh, well, 'bye, then." Her voice reflects the conviction that Morag is very sad that the money didn't turn up. Of course, Charlie says he'll accompany her—well, so what?—and then there's the door shutting and silence.

Appearing immediately would be an admission of eavesdropping. Ted stays imprisoned in the aisles a bit longer before with emerging with his basket.

"Oh, hello, Ted." No acknowledgement from Morag that he'd been the subject of conversation for the last ten minutes.

"Hello, Morag." No acknowledgement from him that he'd overheard it. She rings up his purchases. No acknowledgement that she knows he must have overheard it.

"Dreich day," he says.

"I think it'll brighten up."

"Yes." It's the sort of agreeing remark ordinary people make, even though he doesn't think it will.

But when he gets outside, there's a blue rift in the cloud over Quickly Wood, and the autumn leaves, yellow and orange and red-brown, merge into a glow like sudden golden fire. Yes, that's a cliché, but it happens to fit. They burn with—with what? With a secret you've always wanted to know.

He heads back into the shop, waving the £20 from his back pocket. "Sorry, I forgot. I found this among the cakes."

"That'll be Trish McMenemy's. She thought she lost it when she was buying cakes and things for Leona's birthday party. Excellent."

Heading home, Ted gives a sudden little exhilarated leap and even runs for a few paces. Of course, he is not aware, not really, that three years from now, he and Colin will still live in Arran Rise with many days of blessed humdrum, as when you look out the window and remark that it must have turned cold because Helen McCue has got the hood of her mauve anorak up. Details are even more obscure at the moment: that the spare bedroom will have been colonised by Quickly Computer Support, Colin's own business, doing well in a swathe of villages and small towns outwith the city, and that Ted will be not only two-and-a-half stones lighter but also headmaster of Woodhouse Primary School, where he has inaugurated an annual Easter egg hunt for the pupils in Quickly Wood.

Paul Brownsey

Son House and the Mock Tortoiseshell Beatle Boots

Rob was my Brixton comprehensive
school pal; our friendship forged through
a blues record, Son House and his
12-string guitar:
voice – an anguished cry;
guitar – a scream of pain.

In the school holidays we visited the
West End, browsed guitar shops, coveted
rare records in Dobell's; window shopped
Cecil Gee, with its tab collared shirts,
herringbone tweed jackets,
French denim hipsters.

Anello and Davide, with the handmade
Beatle Boots. I caressed the soft leather –
wanted them.
Bought a pair in the sale;
though garish, mock tortoiseshell,
not black; but wore them, anyway, with my
action painted jeans –
Dad's good gloss paints wasted,
Mum complained.

He's a disgrace, Grandad told her,
on seeing me pass his house,
every evening that summer, on the
way to Brockwell Park;
to gaze at the trees, the sky, the waddling ducks,
the pond of fat goldfish in the walled garden,
the sunflowers –
seeking Blake's 'sweet, golden clime.'

Lone men followed me; police cars cruised;
Mum and Dad confronted me with
Grandad's complaints.
The boots became scuffed and battered;
stained and tattered.

I picked up my chipped, second-hand guitar,
slid the bottleneck over the strings, made
them cry – a scream of pain.

David Danbury

Introduction

I remember no rain, no ankle pain.
I do not recall which Beacon we climbed
on those Malvern Hills, nor that damp bracken.

I don't remember those other walkers
in cagoules, was there a collie too? Why
were we not sure over that path that forked?

Nor the buildings raked like gravel far below,
runnelled by roads. Perhaps, the rich silence
of a pair of raptors soaring on thermals?

Allegro

All that endures in my mind's eye, denuded
of texture, held fast against hurried days,

is one unharried moment: rediscovering
love, a hundred storeys above Sunday.

On our indelible route together.

Clifford Liles

I remember the moon; I remember it stalking the car,
keeping pace over ghostly haystacks, fields and houses.
I remember when the moon lit up the garden
and the apples in the apple tree became, somehow, mythic.
I remember looking through my father's binoculars
seeing those cratered scars, that tranquil sea.
I remember how it lit you up, that other night, naked and cool.
How you seemed different, free; beyond this world.

But that was a long time ago and the dead lie
buried, beneath so many others.
And to be honest, I had almost forgotten.
Until last night, when that same light
came through the un-shuttered window
and as if offering permission, somehow put
a perfect square, of blank page, on the kitchen wall.

Knotbrook Taylor

HONEYMAN

Bert spoke like a character from a Hardy novel,
Dorset in his bones.
He always arrived with jars of liquid gold,
clunks of amber comb oozing honey
from perfectly made hexagonals.

How I loved to eat those
shapes the bees created
flying out from hives into wild fields
to return with bellies full of nectar,
panniers full of pollen.

Then one year he didn't visit,
old age or death.
I still remember this man
who once lived next door to my father
back in those days that are history.

Sue Moules

UFFERN
GWAEDLYD

Something made me look up
and there was my father
running out of the water at Swansea Bay
on Christmas Eve, aged nine,
yelling *uffern gwaedlyd, uffern gwaedlyd,*
till his mother, a waiting towel-matador,
cuffed his head with her elbow,
told him not to speak lowliness
what with Jesus on the way.
Further off, his father watched the others
haring up the shingle with worse on their lips,
pointed his stick at each in turn
like a Maesteg judge grading cattle
and cried *Jiw, Jiw, boys, that is quite enough.*
Then they were off
to a house built of washdays
and what was for them a slap-up meal
whose aromas broadened like magic webs
across the distempered ceiling.

I met my grandparents just a time or two
in rooms almost dark
but for anxious, prodding flames
that sketched their skin wizened
and pressed coal-black eyes deep into their heads.
I met my father a time or two as well
between his engagements with Arms and Crowns
and … the crimper, was it, on the side?
No, the chauffeuse. The crimper was long afterwards,
thickening the shadows beyond his final bed.

When free he would loom at the evening table,
ask me, *How was your day, lad, in all?*
like he was fresh in from the Spanish Main
and I'd been patient on a spit of cliff,
hopping from foot to foot,
hoisting a lamp to the stars.

Uffern gwaedlyd:
(Welsh) Bloody
hell. *Jiw, Jiw:*
(Welsh) Good
heavens! A
softening of 'Duw'
(God) to sound less
blasphemous.
(With thanks to
Sharon Larkin.)

Now, when I picture my father,
he looms just so as I'm sat small
but I see nothing of the chauffeuse-man,
only a nine-year old
uffern-ing up the beach
and, waiting with a tut, a tear,
towel wide as a muzzle-catch,
my mother.

Michael W Thomas

23

A MEMORABLE LESSON
"That was a memorable day to me, for it made great changes in me."
(Charles Dickens: Great Expectations)

Above our desks, dust motes dance in the sun.
At my new grammar school, the autumn term begins
With a first composition, completion in an hour.
The theme, our summer holidays just past,
Reporting on the most noteworthy episode.

I think about one day at our local swimming baths,
My father well enough for once to keep me company,
The pool chill in the open air, and shows me how
To dive, swim under water, open-eyed, and blossom
From timid tadpole to a near frog-like freedom.

He has heavily muscled shoulders, a hairy pelt,
But for a puckered patch below his shoulder blade,
Where once a bullet left his body, a J-shaped scar
From breastbone past his navel, across his abdomen,
Gall bladder missing, part of his stomach taken out.

And then there's me, a little sprat, my shoulders bony,
Painfully thin but lively, with all my ribs on show.
I feel secure, watched by his one good eye,
Forget untried abilities, though at the time I have
No words for love, nor find them in my essay.

After the usual wait, our work books are returned,
One of my classmates singled out for praise
Is told to read aloud his confident account
About an outing to a great naval monument,
Whose tower dominates the country's biggest river.

My stumbling essay handed back, comments in red,
'There's no event of note in what you've written here,
The afternoon described completely unremarkable.'
Sixty years later they return, unbidden – still no appeal
Against this kind of verdict, the utterance of power.

Wilf Deckner

Infinite III

These days everyone is talking about Beeching and the railways that are closing down because of his report. Those of us who travelled on the railways at their worst, during wartime, are tempted to say good riddance to them. Today people get annoyed if their train or bus appears ten minutes late. They cannot imagine what it was like then.

Donald McBeath was a distant cousin of mine. I last met him in 1947 at a family wedding. I've no idea what happened to him afterwards or even where he is now, but we got on well enough then for him to tell me his story. And the thing I remember most vividly about it is the nightmare train journey he described.

He was serving in the Royal Navy in 1941, with honour; distinguished war service, promotion, even medals. He hadn't been home to Scotland since before the war; his ship was based at Portsmouth and that's a long way from Graysfoot in Lanarkshire. In March, however, he was sent on a course in London, something to do with new navigational equipment. It was a two-day affair but his captain, seeing the strain he was under, said, 'Take some extra days. Be back here on the 15th. We're refitting so we won't be sailing till then at least.'

The course finished on the 12th. If he caught an early train next morning he could make it back to Graysfoot to spend a night with his family, travelling back south the following day. He'd have to look out the address. The family had been moved when much of the village was taken over by the army; they tested artillery equipment by firing shells into old pit bings. Some older miners' rows had been refurbished for the displaced families to move into.

Now, gifts for the family? He bought some good pipe tobacco and a leather pouch for his father, who worked at one of the local mines. His mother was easy – he found some balls of quality wool in a craft shop. She loved her knitting. Sam, his younger brother, wouldn't be home, as he'd recently started his army basic training. His sister, Jean, would now be sixteen. What on earth could he get for her?

Leaving the craft shop he bumped into a thin, shifty man who looked at his uniform with suspicion. 'Something for the lady, guv?' the man asked, slyly, half-opening his overcoat.

A thought struck Donald. 'Have you *nylons*?'

'Yeah, 'course.' The overcoat was opened out fully and the goods were extracted. 'Luvly seams on 'em, guv.' Donald bought four pairs. If Jean was half the aspiring lady she'd been when she was 14, she'd love them.

It was a quiet night in London so there was no rush to the shelters and Donald had a decent night's sleep. In the morning he took a bus to Euston and there found a train that left not long after ten. It was busy and noisy and reeking with cigarette smoke and unwashed bodies. At first there were no seats and he made himself comfortable in a corridor with his kitbag as a pillow. The train did not speed north as it would have done four years earlier. Instead it took a tortuous route, leaving the main line clear. Even in quieter backwaters it was held up to let through more important trains. As it trundled into Birmingham by another forgotten side-route, large numbers of people began packing up to leave. Donald was able to dash into a non-smoking compartment and claim a seat by the window. The train remained in Birmingham for nearly an hour. Even after his restful night, Donald's head grew thick and heavy. As the train pulsed again into sluggish life, he slipped into sleep.

When he awoke it was near-dark; there were only faint nightlights in the compartment. He peered out of the window past the blackout blind; the train was stationary with a goods yard alongside. The only brightness came from searchlights probing the heavens for Heinkels. A respectable middle-aged couple now shared the compartment with him.

'Where are we? Are we in Scotland yet?'

'No,' said the woman, 'we're in Lancashire somewhere, I think.'

Her husband looked at her angrily. 'Careless talk!'

'Don't be daft. He's in the Royal Navy.'

'His accent. He's *foreign*.'

'He's *Scottish*, Mortimer. They're on our side.'

The husband kept aloof but Donald chatted with the woman. Earlier they had seen some bombs exploding, she said. The train driver was probably waiting to make sure it was safe to continue. Indeed, a few minutes later the train rattled back into life.

There were more interruptions. Approaching one town – Donald thought it might have been Lancaster, or perhaps Penrith – they stopped again and he was sickened to see distant silent flashes of bombs exploding. The last part of the journey seemed interminable as the train wound slowly through the Borders in the gloom of wartime countryside. He had the compartment to himself, now, the prim couple having left at Carlisle. On the approach to Motherwell the train stopped again. There was little to see eastwards from the compartment window, so Donald went into the corridor to look west.

The distant sky, rather north of west, flickered a sickeningly vivid yellow-orange. Somewhere over there is getting a pasting tonight, he thought.

When the train finally shuddered to a halt at Glasgow Central it was just before six. Twenty hours! At this rate he'd struggle to get back to Portsmouth by the fifteenth unless he turned right round and got the next train south. He decided to keep going; he wanted to see his family, and if he was late back – well, the medals must count for something. He was hardly a deserter.

In the early morning gloom of Gordon Street he could taste burning on the breeze that blew in from the west. Fire engines and ambulances dodged the early trams and buses in Renfield Street. As he waited to cross, an old man in a bunnet and overcoat nodded at one clanging ambulance and said, 'They say Clydebank got hit bad last night.'

The streets were busy even at this early hour as people made their way to work. The light was beginning to gleam in the east by the time he reached Buchanan Street Station. He found a man in a railway uniform and asked when the next train to Graysfoot was.

'There's a Stirling train at seven. It'll get ye there. Mind, we've heard of strays falling as far east as Cumbernauld. Don't be surprised if yer train is held up.'

I was gripped by this part of Donald's story. I remembered that awful night. I lived in Strathblane then, a quiet village north of Glasgow, squeezed between the Campsie Fells and the Kilpatrick Hills. Yet death came to us that night when a stray fell on some cottages and killed two families.

Donald settled in the train which soon cleared the tunnel into grey light at St Rollox. The morning was misty, but there was so much smoke the two seemed to mingle and merge. As the train left the city behind and entered a landscape of clanking pithead machinery, he pondered his next problem and looked at the last letter from his mother. The address was 5 Robert Owen Row, Graysfootmuir. He vaguely remembered the place, once-abandoned dwellings with sharp-toothed broken windows beneath pit bings like black Alps. He'd played among them as a child.

The train arrived at Graysfoot just before eight. The train steamed away leaving a station ghostly in mist tainted with burning and death. A few people, some of them in uniform, stood on the other platform yet there was an acute sense of loneliness; the bustle of Euston Road or Renfield Street seemed a long time ago. He crossed the station forecourt, wisps of smoky mist tugging at him as he went. He could hear the distant sound of pithead gear and of waggons being shunted. To the north the Campsie Fells soared, their summits swaddled in mist; to the west there was a miasma of smoke. He stood there alone, trying to remember the way to Graysfootmuir.

And then a man appeared.

Donald didn't see where he'd come from. It was as if he was newly-formed from smoke and mist. He was tall, taller than Donald, but older and wore a grey overcoat and a grey Brodie helmet. Donald couldn't see any military symbols on the coat.

'Where are you headed, son?' The voice was quiet, hollow, but not hostile.

'Graysfootmuir,' said Donald. 'I'm on leave, and my family have moved there.'

The man looked at Donald, saying no more. Feathers of mist curled between them.

'It's been a bad night,' the man said, finally.

'So I gather,' said Donald. 'It's Robert Owen Row I'm after.'

'Robert Owen Row,' said the man. 'You want to go there?'

Donald began to lose patience. 'Can you tell me which road to take?'

The man pointed vaguely and gave some terse instructions. Donald thanked him and walked in the direction indicated. After he had gone about a hundred yards he looked back over his shoulder and saw no sign of the man. The mist had reclaimed him.

It only took ten minutes to walk to the row. The single-storey terrace emerged suddenly from the mist and he quickly found Number 5 and banged on the door. There was no answer, so he went straight in. Doors were never locked here.

His mother was in the scullery. She came through when she heard him and said, 'Och, it's yourself,' still drying a cup with the teatowel in her hand. Donald smiled; the understatedness of his people! It was as if he'd just nipped out twenty minutes before. His fellow officers from England would be embracing their mothers by now.

Soon he was settled in an armchair with a cup of tea in his hand. His mother sat opposite him in her usual smart blouse and skirt hidden by a pinnie. She never seemed to wear anything else but they never seemed to wear out. 'Your father's on early shift. Jean's at her pal's just now. She's been applying to work in munitions. We got a letter from Sam just the other day.'

They talked on and talked on, and the morning seemed to pass quickly and the mist clear outside. Donald mentioned the bombing at Clydebank and then remembered the man at the station. He described him but his mother shook her head and said, 'That could be anybody, son. Maybe he was a ghostie right enough.'

His mother's thoughts seemed to be elsewhere; that would be the war. The marathon train journey began to tell on Donald and he started to nod. 'Och, away and sleep, son,' said his mother, her voice seeming to come from another room, 'ye've earned it.'

He woke up suddenly, aware that he was cold and that he was being shaken and shouted at. 'What are ye doing here, ye daftie?' came an old man's voice. He opened his eyes, rubbed them, and looked around.

He was in the charred shell of a building, bombed and burnt out; blackened timbers dripped with sooty water. The cottages on either side were less damaged, as if only a stray had landed. He looked at the man stooped over him. He wore a private's Home Guard uniform and he recognised him as Jim Forrester, a pal of his Dad's who had retired from the pit with ill-health a few years earlier.

'Jim, Jim, it's me, Donald.'

The man stopped shaking him. 'Och so it is. I never knew ye were back, son, I'm sorry about…'

'Never mind – where's my mother? She was here. Did the Germans come back?'

'Naw, son, the Germans have no been seen since last night, thank Goad. But why did ye climb in here and lie doon and…'

'I didn't. I got off the seven o' clock train from Buchanan Street. My mother was here but father was on early shift. Jean wasn't here. If this is still the fourteenth the Germans *must* have come back. I *spoke* to her this morning. *All morning.*'

'It's the fourteenth right enough son, but all morning? It's no even nine o' clock yet. Mr Gardner sent us over to see if ye were all right. We were here about two in the morning when the stray landit…'

A light went missing from Donald's eye. The man shouted to his comrades, 'Get Mr Gardner! And get this man to the camp.'

A suburb of army huts now adjoined Graysfoot. One large hut served as a basic infirmary for the camp but had been pressed into use for local victims of bombing. Donald felt uncomfortable about taking up a bed. If there was anything wrong with him, it was in his head.

The man sitting by his bed introduced himself as Samuel Gardner, Civilian Manager at Graysfoot Artillery Testing Station. He was no longer wearing a greatcoat but Donald had no difficulty in recognising the man from outside the station.

'I wasn't sure whether you knew about the bomb at Robert Owen Row, Mr McBeath. I'm sorry if I was a bit guarded and I'm really sorry about your loss. Twenty minutes after you left me I met the Home Guard lads and I sent some of them over in a car to see if you were all right.'

'But I *saw* her. I spoke…'

Gardner clapped him on the shoulder and left.

Donald was in the hospital for just a day. He arrived back at Portsmouth early on the sixteenth of March after another wearisome journey involving three trains. In the circumstances, the Royal Navy would have let him stay in Scotland longer but he couldn't bear to. There were scarcely any remains to bury, anyway.

He slept most of the journey back. At one point he woke, with the train trundling through the Midlands with the oily Trent running outside. He felt inside his coat pocket and pulled out Jean's stockings, the ones he'd bought for her. He sat staring at them for a while, and, when the people sitting opposite began to give him strange looks, he shoved them back in his pocket.

As I said, I have not seen Donald since our talk, but I have met Sam. He married a friend of mine. He, too, had lost touch with his brother, but when I asked what he knew about Donald's tragic journey home, he looked blank. In all the time they were still in touch, Donald had never told him the story. Yet he had told *me*.

It's my only real secret then, and I have shared it now.

David McVey

DID YOU HAVE A GOOD WAR?

They had a good war.
They saw it coming in the tea leaves.
They remained civilians.
Watched the front from way up the back.

He had a good war.
Black market turkey bound and gagged on the table.
Hard times, desperate measures.
Abstention on philosophical grounds and a bad dose of the sky sickness.
Send the lesser men as gun fodder.

She had a good war.
She knew a last minute marriage wouldn't last.
She said she'd wait but found she couldn't.
Those not fit to fight soon rallied round.

We had a good war.
This time it's a laser-guided blitzkrieg.
We rehearsed our pin numbers, turned them into catchy mantras.
Seems the clever money is redesigning the world.
Laying it to waste.
Putting it to rest.

Have a good war.
Forget it's going on.
Take up kite-surfing, lick salt from your lips.
Believe that love brings in the tide.
Lie down on your board.
The ocean is what it is, does what it does, taking no heed of politics.
Float on the lack of a need to know.

I had a good war.
I came back with an interesting skill-set.
Perfect for urban survival.
Highly sought after in the world of skull-duggery.

So let's have a good war.
Let's lie through our teeth.
Wait, collaborate, capitulate.
A couple of years after the enemy have brought us to the bargaining table
they will have become just like us.
We will have become just like them.

Steven Sivell

MOHINI

1

Rarely did she get late mornings or evenings
between ten and half ten and then at half four,
seldom did she take an off, sick day or Sunday
even once-a-year *Holi* in the month of March
didn't hold out a stay-away for Mohini.
She was there to clean, mop, scrub floors and
do a sinkload of dishes twice a day.
Brass and steel pots, spatulas and ladles stacked on one side
porcelain plates, serving bowls and ramekins
making a small knoll to the other side of the sink.

When Mohini entered the kitchen
a succession of smooth moves unfurled.
She took off her wrap, tucked in her *shalwar*,
rolled up her sleeves, turned the gas-hob on
and quick squirts of warm water
flowed over tumblers, tureens and bigger bowls.
She lathered them with an amber liquid detergent
until, in a little while, they were all draped in sparkles,
resting in their grooves and perches on the dish rack
ready for their brief orchestral glory
before the metal hillocks on the neighbouring rack
outshone the delicate music-makers with their glinting clanks,
steely thumps and brass thunders.

Summers, springs and sloshy monsoons
years, decades and a quarter of a century
saw Mohini work on and on and on.

2

I don't understand what Mohini does, my Grandma used to say. No
rubbing, no scouring, no exerting her muscles. Without that, how does
metalware cleanse and shine? What is she up to? Simply holding a pot
under the tap! Hardly have the detergent bubbles slid down when the
utensil bangs down straight onto the draining board. No thorough rinsing,
no final wipe with her hand. A lightning flick if she sees me watching and
that's the end of it. She thinks I don't know what good washing-up is.
Doing dishes, cooking, cleaning, laundry and what not – that's all my life
has been till my eyesight went down and then other parts started to creak
and crumble.

3

There were days when I would perch on the kitchen counter
watch her surreal strokes
now here, now there
now somewhere else altogether
her consummate skill at neatest swipe on a dish
the flick and flip of a bowl
the brisk whisk to the rack.

Mohini auntie, how do you make dishes dance in your hands? A rapid jab
of the soapy fluid on a greasy pan, a snap of your fingers, a runnel of water
cascading down the shiny steel colander and the dish all cheery and
spruced on the stand. How do you do this in the blink of an eye?

For some reason, she always called me by the nickname my brother had
given me.

Rani, when you have to do dishes in six households, sweep and mop in five
of these, do piles of laundry thrice a day for big families, you learn to
squeeze the drippy dishcloth, flick it on cutlery, glasses and plates, rinse
under a gentle stream of water and dab the edges of sink and draining board
dry. Skill arises, my dear, from struggle, and necessity polishes it.

4

On chilly mornings
Mohini placed a pan of piping hot water
close to the sink
rinsed oil-smeared pots, butter dishes,
milk cans and *ghee* containers,
drained the pan, re-filled it,
dipped more utensils, stack by stack,
thawing stains and splodges
and then started the regular washing up.

There simply wasn't room enough
in our sink one morning
pots, frying pans and serving bowls
had trailed down to the floor
and made quite a crescent in front of the unit.

Mohini had taken a day off
the flu though was a minor ordeal
the bigger bother was how efficiently

a mere twenty four hours had swelled the workload.
All the sinks she tackled that day
showed up mounting piles of utensils
taller and heftier than their usual size.
No sighs, no phews, no dropping of mute mugs,
Mohini got on with sluicing the suds
without losing time or patience or wasting her breath.

5

Mohini always dressed in pastels
with the cleanest white wraps around her shoulders
a plain iron loop sitting around her right ring finger
on her left a brass ring worn down to a sheenless band.
Toes spliced on plastic slippers
feet spread out wide as if they had to hold fast
lest the slipper should slip away.
Autumns, blistering noons and misty onsets of winters
saw Mohini's footwear, wrap and her no-nonsense plait
remain the same as they had always been.

6

Mohini auntie, why do you have these deep green-grey bits permanently
lodged under your fingernails and toe-nails? Can't you scoop it out, once
and for all, with the curvy hook of a nail clipper? Should I give you
Mum's? She won't mind at all.

Well, Rani, when hands and feet remain in water sixteen out of twenty four
hours a day, they develop this grey-green goo – dirt, detergent, dead skin
and bits of ash I rub on bronze bowls for extra shine. Your Grandma insists
I do it. All this makes a gunge that's hard to get rid of. Besides, who knows
what all seeps into my skin as I scrub and sweep.

Mohini auntie, please use Mum's hand lotion. It'll make these tough
wedges soften and ooze away soon. Shall I fetch it for you?

She smiles and shakes her head, as usual.

7

I may leave wads of banknotes on my bedside table, Mum used to say, or
drop my diamond ring on the floor, or Rani may take off her gold-studs
and leave them with jackstones in the verandah, or Amar uncle's gold tooth
may come loose in a bowl of *daal* as it did the last time he had lunch with

us. No matter what, Mohini will retrieve it and, without any fuss, hand it to me. A rarity our Mohini is. So rich in integrity despite her circumstances.

8

And then the day Mohini gave up work.
Her sons didn't want her to clean and mop any more,
her daughters-in-law promised to support and take care of her.
Mohini made up her mind
and chose to go by the family decision.

As she took leave of Grandma and Mum,
she held my hand in both of hers.

Dearie, I didn't tell you frankly the other day. Under my fingernails resides Bahawalpur, the homeland I left behind in Pakistan. My town. The mango and guava orchards my siblings and I would sneak in. The sweetmeat shop near our house. The Lal Suhanra Park we would sometimes go to. And the friends I played with. Yes, in 1947, we became independent but the dislocation overshadowed everything. From free India to humanity to future. We all yearn to be free but freedom remains a chimera for the poor.

And so Mohini left with an unblinking gaze
unassuming dignity from head to toe
and the natural wave of her black hair
with few flecks of grey.

Jaspreet Mander

On day one...

We are graced by veteran publishers of poetry and stories deemed too niche to sell, but sell in defiance nonetheless. Writers with their prayers, that history is a living thing, that even the everyday person can craft a tale our world should hear. We arch our necks towards cinema screens, watch as each photo of a life lived flickers from projected light, laugh in unison at the comedy of fathers playing in sand. We listened as poets in Trinidad and pop stars are cradled into their beds with the care of callused hands holding a book, with the pride of their first published poetry collection, radiant. We are off to a good start!

On day two…

We share chocolates and food amongst the tech-weary, exchange notes and poetry collections to read. I photograph a stained-glass window as that brief winter sunlight fades. I am fighting the urge to buy fish and chips, sharing this radiant chips revolution as workers strike. Later on, it's pride and prison, creative rage against the cage; rainbow flags against the haters, pride in who we are. Up next, we contemplate the future and look back to those who came before; pioneers against a future fixed as outside kids chat about cheese and space.

On day three…

Last night I dreamt of sound dealers, a symphony of electric hums from streetlights and serene smoky custard was like fog across empty fields. It's very possibly I may have devoured too much sugar or perhaps a poem gone very wrong. This morning was silent, too silent and my voice echoed back through speakers with its two-way microphone signal. Then a politician appeared out of thin air, moments after we conversed about the impermanence of social media. Photos taken, tables of fish and chips consumed. Today so far has been quiet, relaxing. Post-performance skills workshop, there's an open mic; the stage is ready, the audience awaits.

On day four…

Today's weather began with a bone-chilling cold. Now is the moment for coated layers to descend. I am eager to listen again, too eager it seems; I am one hour early. The studio is silent. This silence is broken by songs of home and a plastic fox, teas on tap and a plate of tempting chocolate digestives. Crunch. Our cups clang and we toast you, the participants; in a world of impermanence and digitally crafted creations, we own this. For the first time since the pandemic years our hall is busy with performers conversing in a clash of stories. On the background speakers, a classical waltz plays for us. We dance with joy. I have made new friends today. I am cold no more.

On day five…

It began with a lazy afternoon; we are starting to run on fumes or at least the few of us that avoid energy drinks for obvious reasons. And our creative director Tony celebrates their birthday! On our internet radio a tale of homelessness and compassion is told as we discuss the history of Writing on Air. Soon a crowded room, a ruckus of writers, and tower of songs. We end this evening with champagne and a toast to a job well done. Well met, my friends. Writing On Air 2022 is a resounding success.

Jaimes Lewis Moran

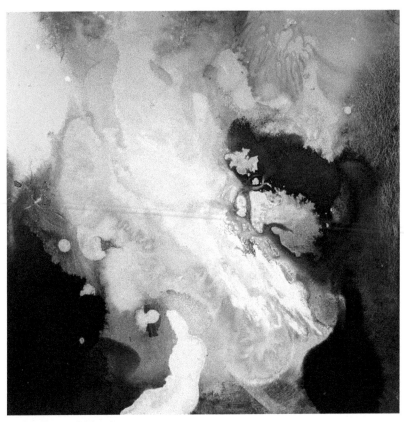

Reflections of Clouds

1. At some point during your walk through the woods, stop and listen and look. What bird is that singing, what can you smell, what lingers behind that tree, what is on your mind?

2. Always use a small notebook, pencil or pen, a recorder, or a palace of memory. Go sit in a coffee shop, on a mountain top, a graveyard. Be by an ocean, a window, or maybe just a beetroot, lying quietly by the kitchen sink.

3. Blow up the town hall, murder your mother, develop the ability to fly using only feathers found on the forest floor, turn into a wolf on the full moon; but don't do all these things at the same time.

4. Speak about love without using the word love.

5. If you are going to a party: don't be the first to arrive. Always leave before you get so drunk, that you begin to repeat yourself.

6. Things in poems are never cerulean blue or turquoise, they never break into shards, they are never clever cards, kept close to the chest. In this light you should wear a plain pair of glasses to help others to see.

7. Bondage and discipline can be a good, if you like that sort of thing; tying down words to a frame, or merely limiting their freedom, can sometimes make them confess.

8. Don't believe the lie that nobody is interested in you, or your life. When you start to tell your story, this is the only thing they will really want to know.

9. If you find yourself in a box, that's okay, you can always step out; to where you are a god. Soon you will realise; there is truth but, on the other hand, there is *truth*.

10. Finally, remember, because we never said there'd be no pain, the best poems, the very best poems, hide in the dark with the monsters inside you …

Knotbrook Taylor

THE WHOLE IS GREATER THAN THE SOME OF ITS POETS

Some poets look better on the page
Some poets sound better on a stage
Some poets are red with rage
Some poets are beige
Some poets are the sage of the age
(Motion, Duffy, Armitage)
Some poets   do
stuff   like   this
  which   goes   right   over
                                                    my
                                                    head

Some poets are dead.

Simon Tindale

FAREWELL

A rose the colour of brandy
drops one petal, then another.
The water glass holds
a tiny window pane.

Clouds move and light
shifts. The sky casts a
mauve shadow
on the smoothed sheet.

Here is my dying friend.
Nothing lasts; the forty years
fold up. Already they've
shouldered their pack and gone.

Paula Jennings

The spot is marked by a 12 foot obelisk composed of lava rocks. Melted earth. The area of the crater is surrounded by a barbed wire fence. In one direction is a mountain wall. The rest of the landscape is barren desert. A truly remote location. After more than 75 years, the area is still slightly radioactive.

Before Hiroshima, before Nagasaki, there was Trinity. On the morning of July 16, 1945, the world's first nuclear device was exploded in the remote desert of New Mexico. As the morning sky was rent by the explosion, J. Robert Oppenheimer recalled the lines from the Bhagavad Gita – "Now I am become Death, the destroyer of worlds."

It was a destination I knew I would have to visit in my travels. I would have to stand in the spot where the human animal, unique among the beasts, had become capable of causing its own extinction.

I stopped in Socorro, New Mexico, about thirty miles northwest of the Trinity site. In a roadside diner, I met an old timer who had been alive at the time of the blast. He told me about the night it had occurred, when the sky was a bath of white and the sound of thunder had come tearing across the desert. A few weeks later he heard about Hiroshima and Nagasaki and knew what that night had wrought.

He spoke of going to the Trinity Site as a child and collecting strange chips of stone, altered by the blast, a substance that would later be called trinitite. Then the government had arrived and cordoned off the area. He related tales of protesters who occasionally came with signs, protesting the atomic bomb, or wars, or nuclear power, or the use of the bomb at Hiroshima, or Trinity itself. And he said the people of his generation had suffered "a lot of ailments" through the years, from living so close to the bomb site. But it never occurred to him to move. This was his home. This was all he knew. To him, an atom bomb might go off in your neighborhood when you're a child. It's just a part of life.

The Trinity Site is deep inside the White Sands Missile Base. I had to pass through a barbed-wire gate and show photo identification. I was told to drive about 17 miles down a desert road until I came to the Permanent High Explosive Testing Area. I was then to turn left. I was worried I might miss the turn, but there was no chance of that. When I reached the fork in the road, an armed soldier stood sentry, making certain I didn't accidentally stray into the Permanent High Explosive Testing Area. He didn't feel half as strongly about it as I did.

After driving another five miles, I could see the obelisk in the distance, surrounded by a large, circular barbed wire fence, the size and shape of the blast crater. I had to exit my car and pass on foot through another guarded gate.

I stood where Oppenheimer had stood, and Fermi and Teller. There were those who had chosen not to come, like Leo Szilard, who did not want to witness what they had done.

In the final days before the detonation, a macabre humor had developed among the scientists. They had organized a betting pool to predict the size of the explosion. General Groves received disturbing reports from the Army guards—Enrico Fermi was taking side bets on whether they would accidentally ignite the atmosphere and end all life on the planet.

The device was placed on a metal grate tower with wires leading to various measuring devices. The scientists set it off just before dawn.

It has been called "The Day the Sun Rose Twice."

An atomic tourist who looks carefully on the ground can still see examples of trinitite, a substance that doesn't exist anywhere else in the world. It was created when the nuclear explosion fused the desert sand of New Mexico. A piece of trinitite is about a centimeter wide. The top surface is smooth and green. The bottom is light gray and rough and looks like concrete. The most common form of trinitite is green, but there is also black, red, and blue. Black trinitite contains occlusions of iron from the tower which held the device. Red trinitite is caused by the fusing of copper from the wires that were run from the bomb to the various measuring devices. No one knows what causes blue trinitite. It is illegal to remove a piece of trinitite from the area. All trinitite is radioactive.

After absorbing enough history, and probably more than enough radiation, I got back into my car and headed toward the state highway, glad to leave the Trinity site in my rearview mirror.

H.G. Wells, one of history's seminal thinkers, had thought the tank so horrific—as it rolled insensate across the bodies of dead and wounded soldiers and civilians, as it destroyed fields, and ruined villages—that the world would be unable to face the horrors of such a monstrous weapon and would be forced to put an end to war once and for all. The thinkers of an earlier generation had believed the same thing about the rapid-fire Gatling gun. The next generation would hold the same belief about the atomic bomb.

I imagine that somewhere in our dim, dark past, a cave philosopher noticed that the attacking tribe was swinging sticks, and thought, "This can't go on!"

After making his name and fortune writing prophetic tales of science fiction, H.G. Wells turned his great mind to anti-war activism and spent the latter part of his life trying to save the world.

He didn't realize the world doesn't want to be saved.

When the earliest human discovered he had an opposable thumb, the first thing he made was a fist.

Mark Pearce
Re-printed here, with apologies to Mark for typos in DC 46, which crept in during the processing.

After six Official Earth weeks, they had still not decided on Night.

Gil, whose mother owned the company funding the consortium paying the sub-contractors, convened a meeting of the Settlement Council. The four of them sat at the round table in the new, high-domed Council Chamber.

Loveign, Councillor for Engineering, puffed at her herbal pipe and said, "Do we actually *need* Night? The cost will be ridiculous. After all, people are able to adjust the lighting and temperature in their own domiciles. They can make it dark whenever they want."

Trinber, Councillor for Socio Medico Ethics, barked, "Circadian rhythms. For the first time in our history, humans are on a planet with no Night. Not even twilight. Not even a slight dusk. Without Night, the Settlers may go mad." He scowled at Loveign. "And that will cost a damn sight more than a bit of CGI."

Loveign scowled back. "Which is why I strongly advised against landing here in the first place. Totally impractical." She sighed. "But apparently practicalities mean nothing against the beauty of the three suns, the majesty of the purple mountains, yada yada yada yada yada. People don't all have the same Circadian rhythms though, do they? Why can't they just turn the bloody lights off when it suits them?"

"I think," said Genmore, Councillor for Mytho Religio Experience, "you are overlooking the shared Mytho Religio significance of Night as a Mytho Religio phenomenon."

Loveign clenched her pipe with her teeth. "In humanspeak?"

Genmore smiled at her beneficently, steepling his fingers beneath his chin. "Night is more than just not-day, Loveign. Night is a feeling. It is the unknown, the thing from which light protects us. The recognised *otherness* of Night is one of the things that bind our species together."

"As is the ability to turn off a light switch," said Loveign. "And the archives show that by the time of the Great Evacuation human beings had all but destroyed Night, along with everything else. In most places, Night was as bright as day. Our ancestors liked to see where they were going."

Trinber said, "Genmore's point, which I accept may be difficult for the mechanistic mind to understand, is that human psychological and emotional well-being is intimately connected with being in tune with our natural environment. Including Night."

Loveign laid her pipe on the table. "But," she said, "we are on a planet with no natural Night. How can we be in tune with our environment if we alter one of the fundamental aspects of the fucking thing?"

There was a moment's crystalline silence.

Genmore's voice was icy. "You seem to have forgotten, Loveign, that it was unkindness and disrespect, and not the inability to see where you were going, that killed the great Earth civilisations."

"Alright, we need a vote," said Gil briskly. "Mother wants this sorted. Those in favour of adding Night to the settlement and bringing forth proposals for funding of same? Thank you. Those against? Duly noted, Loveign. Motion carried."

"Then you better explain to *Mother*," said Loveign bitterly, "that my budget won't cover it." She nodded at Genmore and Trinber. "And I can't see them offering to cover the engineering costs."

An Information Notice duly went out on all channels, assuring settlers that Night was in development and medication was available from registered pharmacies for adverse effects on Circadian or other rhythms in the meantime. There was little reaction one way or the other until the fringe political group DELME put out its own notice querying the purpose of the Night project.

"NIGHT," it boomed, "may be part of human inheritance, but what kind of NIGHT is this Council, made up of the elite and privileged whose forbears got their places in the Evacuation through connections, not merit – what kind of NIGHT will they inflict on us? And what will they use it for?"

Over the next few Official Earth days, there were mass demonstrations demanding democratic control of Night development.

Gil summoned D, the main organiser of DELME, who was her brother, to a meeting at the Council Chamber. "What the fuck are you doing?"

D looked hurt. "Carrying out my brief."

"Your brief," said Gil, "is to provide the settlers with a successful subversive and disruptive organisation, thus reassuring them that someone is doing subverting and disrupting so well, *they don't have to*. You're lucky," she continued remorselessly, "that Mother is occupied with enhancing the true human experience on Settlement Eight by creating properly endangered species. What are you and other initials going to do about this?"

D muttered, "It would help if you'd let me have the final plans for Night now, before you go public. Then we could put out identical demands, say you'd agreed to look at them, and then announce we've triumphed and got exactly the Night we wanted."

Gil looked out of the panoramic window.

"So?" said D. "Final plans?"

"Not completely finalised," said Gil.

D raised his eyebrows. "Partially finalised? One iota finalised?"

Gil sighed and turned back to face him. "Genmore and Trinber have been at the archives again. Apparently a proper Earth Night needs animals that only come out at Night, and plants that smell different at Night or only open at Night, or do a dance and howl at the moon at Night. Talking of which, Genmore wants three moons to match the three suns because otherwise it will spoil the symmetry and upset the Mytho Religio experience, while Trinber says three moons will confuse people and do something appalling to their Socio Medico balance, although they seem to manage with three suns. And Loveign just keeps moaning that we can't even afford basic darkness, never mind animals and bushes. And moons." She paused for breath, kneading her forehead with her fingers. "Three hundred years of travelling and settling, and the first time we colonise a planet with no Night, it's on my watch. I just hope those endangered species keep Mother busy for a while."

Two Official Earth days later, the Council reconvened. Trinber, Loveign and Genmore settled themselves in their individually moulded chairs and smiled contentedly at each other across the table.

"What?" said Gil, disconcerted by the curious sight of Loveign's mouth curving upwards. "Why are you all smiling?"

"We've found a way to fund it," said Loveign happily.

"More than fund it," said Trinber, beaming at Gil.

"And we'll have enough left over to fund even more enhancements of the human experience." Genmore looked ecstatic.

Gil eyed them coldly. "You do know that accessing funding outside of approved consortium channels is strictly forbidden?"

Loveign's grin broadened. "Don't worry," she said. "Night will be completely self-funding."

Gil stared.

"The thing about Night," said Genmore, "is that it's dangerous. Partly," he regarded Loveign with something almost like affection, "because you can't see where you're going, but mainly, in a civilised society, because you can't see what's coming."

"I'm not with you," said Gil.

"Nocturnal animals of course," said Trinber, "but, primarily, other humans. Night releases something in humans. They behave differently."

Gil gave an impatient snort. "I'm fully aware that Night will require increases in security forces, artificial lighting and medical facilities. I don't see how all that can be self-funding. Or are you only talking about the immediate engineering costs?"

"No," said Genmore. "We're talking about the lot."

"Do enlighten me," muttered Gil.

"Night falls," said Loveign, her voice sonorous and conspiratorial. "All rules, regulations and boundaries dissolve. Everything feels and sounds…different."

"You should hear Loveign's sound designs," Trinber interrupted excitedly. "Echoing footsteps, rustling bushes, snapping twigs. Completely terrifying."

Gil slapped her hand against the table. "I don't see how a load of aural enhancements is going to solve the funding problem."

"They make it clear what's out there," said Loveign. "They let people know there is real danger in Night."

"But there isn't," said Gil.

"There has to be," said Genmore. "Otherwise it won't work."

Gil looked at him wearily. "What won't?"

"Individual responsibility." Genmore's voice hung in the Chamber. "People have a choice. If they choose to go out and face the danger, they're going to need protection."

"From *what*?" shouted Gil.

Trinber said, "We open the prison hulks and the secure hospital units."

Gil stared at him. "We can't do that."

"As Councillor for Socio Medico Ethics," Trinber said quietly, "I can."

"Eventually," said Genmore, "We may not even need the enhancements. There will be enough real echoing footsteps and rustling bushes to create the necessary demand."

"Demand for *what*?" Gil shouted again.

"Protection!" Loveign shouted back, triumphantly. "People will have a choice. They either stay within their own domiciles during Night, or they buy protection to keep them safe outside." She beamed at Gil. "We're talking alarm devices of varying efficacy, depending on cost. Deterrent devices – sprays, electrical charges and so forth – of varying efficacy depending on cost. Possibly fully functioning weapons of individual destruction, which would always be efficacious, whatever the cost. All manufactured and supplied by the consortium, with a guarantee that a percentage of all profit comes to the Council. Enough to fund Night and a good few other things as well."

After a moment Gil asked, "Suppose they all just decide to stay indoors?"

"But they won't," said Genmore. "Humans are hotwired to be part of a social group. As we know from the archives, isolation has very bad effects on the human psychic process."

"Likewise with physical health," said Trinber.

"Humans just want to be out there with other humans," said Loveign. "Whatever the drawbacks."

Gil's voice was unsteady. "I think this may be contra-human. Mother has always been very insistent that all development must be in keeping with humanity's basic principles. Protecting the community is one of the most basic."

Loveign leaned forward eagerly. "That's the point. Night will bring enormous economic benefits to the community, and the needs of the community always take precedence over the individual. It's a fundamental tenet of the settlements."

Genmore said, "Rest assured, it isn't contra-human. We've checked the archives. The last coherent records we have for Earth, before Panic And

Shitstorm, indicate that most societies encouraged certain citizens to take complete responsibility for their own safety."

Gil frowned. "Certain citizens? Which ones?"

Trinber looked puzzled at the question. "The vulnerable ones, of course. The ones most at risk. Waste of time to encourage the powerful. They already have protection."

Gil said, "You think the settlers will accept this?"

"Oh yes,' said Genmore comfortably. "History shows that if you say something loud enough and often enough, everyone will accept it."

"DELME could be very helpful," Trinber said enthusiastically. "We need them to run another campaign against the Council. You know – how can we trust that elite and privileged lot to keep ordinary people safe, make sure your security stays in your own hands because it's all a plot to control us anyway. That sort of thing."

"The consortium will have a monopoly on supplies," said Loveign, "so it really can't fail. I expect any sceptics will fall straight into line after a few fatalities, or when their neighbours start calling them anti-social and just asking for it, whatever it is. That's certainly what the archives show."

Gil got up and walked to the window. She looked out at the triple suns, the purple mountains, and the settlement replete with promise for its occupants and the generations who would follow them in this astonishing human adventure.

She turned back to the others, beaming. "That's absolutely fucking brilliant," she said. "Mother will be thrilled. So inventive. So efficient. So financially rewarding. So very, very, *very* human."

Jane Ayrie

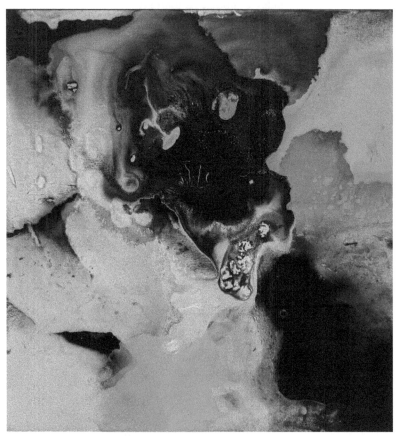

Sun Drenched Reflection

SCALES
GRADE 1 – 8
AND BEYOND

She drops her thumb on middle C,
lets her right hand trickle the keys,
fingers hesitant to press down.

She claws an invisible orange,
C D E thumb under to F,
index G, middle A, fourth B,

gets there with her pinky on C.
It continues, key to key as
she repeats, makes her fingers work.

The repetitive octave climbs,
falls, advances, recedes, swells, fades,
gushes into a torrent of

star-spun rivulets to augment
an ocean, de novo, of pitch,
wave on wave on wave on wave;

Now two octaves, now three, left hand,
right hand, bass clef, treble clef, thirds,
fifths, major, minor, arpeggios,

crescendos, diminuendos –
chromatic dominos toppling
in a drift of black and white tone,

zebras crossing zebra crossings,
again and again and again,
de capo, accelerando,

agito, allegrissimo,
brioso, velocissimo,
and YES! YES! ATLASTISSIMO!

Mozart – Beethoven – Schubert – Liszt –
Blissful melodies flow through her
fingers like shingle song singing

to the beach, while the tide ebbs and
flows in a Sisyphus labour
of ornamental appoggiatura.

Jane Sharp

The old man sits
By the railings,
Pretends to read 'The Times'.

The lunch-hour demob
Filters through,

Intent on escaping office routine.
The old man spies me.
'Max Bruch wrote two more
Violin Concertos,' he says.

'Did you know that?'
I smile,
And continue towards the park.

He page-flicks through 'The Times'.
'Two more concertos,'
He shouts after me –

'Two more.'
I quicken my pace,
Do not look back.

Michael Newman

IS BLUE AN ILLUSION?

in older times there was no colour blue
it was a mystery, a myth
our eyes could not comprehend
our tongues could not distinguish
extending out of green, or a deeper shade of red
like Homer's wine-dark sea
it must have emerged into our consciousness
half-dream, half magic
revelling in the luxury of its newly discovered self
the lapis on the death masks of Egyptian kings
the blue of the virgin's dress
'true blue', the genuine article
loyalty unwavering

it's still with us, that argument of perception
as we bicker over dresses on screens
our apparatus is the same, but varied
like sea glass and ocean current
all the colours of the water
rods and cones and synapses, each telling different tales.
we point at a thing and label it
without knowing if it is truth

I think of Monet and his orange water
how as his eyes deteriorated
they did not present him with a fading world
but one that blazed

Lauren K. Nixon

THE CLOUDS

And when the inevitable clouds come
To cover the pale blue sky
And hide the sun's light
Do not curse them
For though the thunder may shake you
And the lightning shock you
You may forget the rains
And the blessings they give
To nurture our gardens
So that they may be fruitful
You will enjoy the blueness of the sky
A little later in time

Joseph Estevez

A NEAR-DROWNING AND A LIGHTNING RESCUE
'I swam in the thunderstorm' Peter Redgrove, Poet

A lightning fist in a sonic glove jabs the purple eye of the storm.
No bell rings, no ref's gentle shove, no safe laying down of norms

like, "Good clean fight from the off, cease to clinch when I tell you to
part…"
just ungloved knuckles of surf thumping groin and heart.

The boxing ring twists, capsizes, turnbuckles fail, ropes flop aside.
Conger eels grope the victor's prizes. My butterfly stroke won't fly.

Coach is waving a terry towel. *Take a dive! Go! Drop!*
I'm spent. I inhale. I sink. A billion volts rips the ocean top.

Nothing survives of heroes who square up to resist.
I beat the count, win golden gloves by ducking Thor's iron fist.

He lugs me to a placid grove, unbuckles his iconic belt,
fastens it round my embarrassed waist, rubs alive my heart.

Not many know this protector of man, upholder of law.
Despite giant appetites, there is much in him to adore.

If a thunderstorm overtakes you on some bleak moor
lie down near a footing of drystone wall
    and you will have, as I did, a cool encounter with Thor.

Philip Burton

THE FIELD

You might do worse than walk
the short way, across the field,
that white one, with nothing in it,
or the same street again, the stones
strangely familiar, as if a friend
might ever be known, every year
remembered, every day logged
in detail, when the merest scene
escapes the eye, or the words shared
twist in the wind, that what was said
sounds otherwise, as accidence,
time's inflection testing the mind,
that tries to be true, to what was heard,
as were the clouds to pause, the sky
to do your bidding, the street freeze,
or the field to be finally white,
for your words to walk across

Ray Malone

DEVIZES WHITE HORSE

It is possible to stand on the very stone
and be its eye looking over the flat horizon
to the south, the gentle breathing of hills,
smoke snorted from factories and clouds
lugging rain to the coast. All is silent
but for the escalating pinpoint of larks.

It could have cantered across this sweet meadow
of orchids and settled, sweating as if after a race,
oblivious to its power, its own scattered dimension:
ears it cannot fathom, a tail it has never seen,
foreshortened legs too distant to make sense of.
It is a stranger to itself.

And who was there ever to make a whole creature of it
except those who unfolded its blanket of turf
and packed its flanks with chalk? Only they
and the invisible larks and now drivers in the valley
who, caught unawares, find it flashing white
between trees and houses and blithely name it: horse.

Jeff Phelps

unthought of, my hands rest upon
the book I brought that I am ignoring
I want to look *and look and look*

at flashes of bunting strung between dripping trees
at herons on the riverbank
at the sign for Water Orton
at the giant ghost someone painted on a palette and hung
outside their neighbour's window for Halloween
giving the kids a fright

at the graffiti on the wall below a burnt-out roof,
declaring 'HiM bAD' – who, I wonder?
no one left among the charred beams and fallen shingle

at the tiny churches nestled beneath the big city giants,
their glass and steel sparkling like insects
when the sun peeks through storm clouds
that have chased us south

at the flower stall in the station, with a riot of sunflowers and cosmos
at the child in her pram, bouncing the Peppa Pig balloon
that someone has tied to her wrist up and down
up and down
fascination scrunching up her tiny face.

and at the unapologetic words, painted huge and ragged
on the back of a warehouse between Tyseley and Acocks Green:
proudly declaring *VELVET UNDERPANTS* to the world
To the world!

Lauren K. Nixon

Boneless effigies roused into flight
By a temperate breeze, gesticulating freely
In impassioned appeal against some injustice
To the great unseen.
Their limbs loosely tethered – like foreign lands
To imposed ideals of democracy.
They dance, they shake, convulse and fit,
Pegged by wooden manacles
Or gaily-coloured plastic clips.
Drying, waving – legs, socks, sleeves,
Fight so brave to beat air's gong.
Votes made with the boldest cross;
A wasted voice, the contest lost.
Handless, footless, open-necked
– Grasping next-to-nothingness.
Floating mimes – their offerings.

D M Street

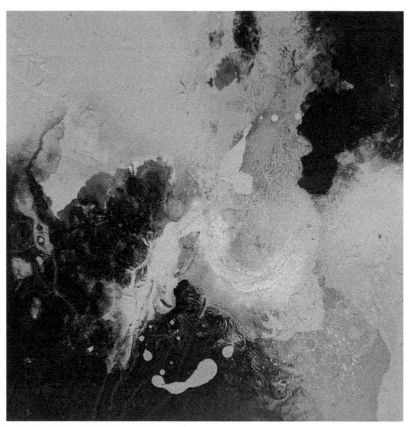

We Met When We Were Almost Young

You thought you'd give it a go – it might be fun. Undemanding work, a little light dusting. References not required – after all they paid a pittance. It was work under the radar. And not like you hadn't done it before; as a student, cleaning flats in London.

For some reason the two interior designers had stuck in your mind; their gorgeous immaculate flat; the variety of cleaning preparations required for doing the bathroom – the creams and powders, the soft cloths to buff it all at the end. Then there were the big substantial semis in north London; the American fridges groaning with food; pate and jellied meat, cheeses and pastries. All in little individual dishes, decorative and delightful. In the student house you'd kept your food in a box, the milk turning rancid. Here – as if everyone was preparing for a siege, an apocalyptic future of shortages and war. You were moved by this display of nurture; salivated sympathetically.

But this would be different. The demographic elderly by definition – people who needed a bit of extra help with housework rather than the time-poor, who could afford to pay for service.

The first client, Gladys; small and spry, sharp tongued – her flat spotless, sparsely appointed with heavy dark furniture. Gladys's passion was cricket, an enthusiasm she had shared with her husband. She'd married late, after working for many years as a matron in the local NHS hospital. You speculated, observing the husband's photo, his unsmiling gaze, that the marriage had been embarked upon as a safety net for his dotage. But Gladys had a different story to tell. Of a husband who morphed into a mad child, hunkered down, squealing like a trapped pig. His sudden demented dark, the mattress flooded each night, parody of a wet dream. His no way back. He'd died shortly after being admitted to a care home.

She was on her own again, game as always, leading her neat respectable life. Containing the shock waves that still ran through her. She shopped, kept clean, put out a briskly cheerful demeanour. But she was diminished. Against expectations she had trusted, taken a chance, married this bluff ex-military man whom she'd met at the cricket club over a G & T. And found the companionship she had tentatively, even fearfully embraced, brutally snatched away.

The kitchen was never used. Gladys seemed to be drying up, desiccating before your eyes. Her comments on current events and gossip became increasingly bitter. Gladys's secret; an ornate box positioned on the glass topped table, its surrounding field of tell-tale crumbs. Sweet detritus, the pink and white coconut ice she fed on as she stood staring out at the cricket field below. The one thing they'd shared; the crack of the bat, a splatter of clapping. Green and balmy evenings.

Then there was Alan – not that you would presume to call him that. His dark dingy apartment in which everything was brown or shades of jaundice. Alan was angry and confused, with leaking eyes, a leg like an exploded sausage.

My wife's in a home, he said, sitting hunched and purple on a seeping leather chair. A stickler for time he'd forget how long you'd stayed, refuse to pay, stare bleakly, head trembling. No sign of her, the woman who was his wife. No clothes or shoes or photographs. When had she left, been sent, taken – which month, which year. You didn't know and you thought Alan didn't know either. Arguing with Alan about money was not a pleasant prospect. There were others after all.

Dorothy was sweet and lived in a purpose-built block looking out onto manicured gardens. Dorothy was powdered and pink. She'd lived with her adored father until he died. Then they said she must sell, there were too many repairs, the dogs and horses all put down. This was confided during the mid-morning cup of tea and she did not weep, was quite matter of fact about it all. Only one pug-like creature remained, wheezing orgiastically into a discarded slipper.

Dorothy was easy to 'do for', undemanding and vague. There was only a bit of washing up and vacuuming of the Chinese rugs – well layered with dog hair. These and the china, all that was left of her inheritance. You frisked round with a duster, appalled by the tray of prescription drugs, the heavy sweetish smell. The rooms were warm, too warm. As if age wrought a terrible penetrating cold, only checked by fug, the comfort of habit.

Elaine lived in a bright high ceilinged flat, the ground floor of a Victorian terrace with its own garden. Elaine was going blind by increments, adrift in a silt of photographs and exquisite objects. Vases and paintings and damask covered chairs; velvet cushions and silk drapes embroidered or deeply hued in jewelled colours. Her beautiful son, long hair, loose shirt open at the throat, laughed up at you from a frame decades old.

There was a daughter, Cecile, back for six weeks for a visit. They never talked about it. That she would leave, return to Melbourne, her own life. That the door would close behind her, the dark deepen. An afternoon when Cecile washed and hulled fresh strawberries, arranging them, huge and fragrant, in a cut glass dish; sprinkled with a sparkle of sugar, enveloped in cream, pearly and rich. She placed the dish on a round table by the garden window – a pleasure for when they returned from their walk in the June sunshine. It would be her last day.

You were left with the washing up, the sweeping; the spoiling red fruit. How the unspoken grief hung like a fog, so you'd choke, blotting up spilled food amid a disorder of fallen objects which slipped and tottered behind Elaine as she stumbled her way through the rooms after Cecile had gone.

Mrs Gordon had the best flat of all of them, on a classic square, the balcony with a sea view. Sometimes you fantasised that she would leave it to you in her will – a moment of untypical gratitude and generosity. This was until you knocked an antique clock off the wall when trying to dust it and the glass face shattered. Her stony condemnation chilling.

Mrs Gordon read the tabloids, gorged on them, spewed her diet of poison and triumph. She was old, old – infinitely furrowed, bony-papery insubstantial. As if only the bile of her habit kept her alive. So she was lit like a gargoyle in her animation, forgetting the failing functions of her body, the weaknesses she did not bear lightly. The tea break was seared with her fury as she sought your complicity in her judgements.

You thought the kingdom of the old was a sour place; the stink of stale breath, a thing that had been kept too long. Let oxygen kill, you thought. The air that we breathe burning us up. Let it be timely.

Denise McSheehy

MIRROR AGREEMENT

I have to buy, or you sell
on the same terms
as triggered by the date.

There's always a time
when it becomes inevitable
and because it's now.

The operative clause
jumps out boldly
from the shadows

of that so long ago deal
we never thought we'd need
but surprised us today.

This is the shoelace
that broke to trip
into the stumble

that still leaves us both
upright. The deal ends
with us mirrored

the only way we can
see each other, and
now forever, ourselves.

Michael Penny

LAIRAGE

When the sheep arrive, they are
Ragged; filthy fleeces half off, half on,
Staring at this strange field. Wary
Of their good fortune in finding so much green.

Some appear to frisk, to imitate
Lambs, but really just to stretch legs.
Most stare about until they are
Chivvied round the field by conscientious dogs.

They stand around in clumps,
Thickets of blank-eyed anxiety, but
Soon enough they find some grass
To sample, and find a semblance of normality.

Within a week, their raggedness is
Vanished from their backs. So smart and spruce
They form up in undulating forage lines
Content to stay a while in this unexpected paradise.

But soon the lorries will come back;
The road clangs with each shit-stained jolt.
Then the well-groomed bodies will march
Smartly, to their rendezvous with the stun gun and the captive bolt.

Edward Alport

No more dead lamb lumps to be coaxed
from a quivering ewe's hot body. Curlew
trills her flute, the shepherd piper
from the hills came down, came years ago;
grey hair fluttering, wind-combed wool on a fence,
eyes, like summer blue, fingering memory's note.
His deep round tongue, true as an old ram's horn,
modulated dialect of stone.

Joe Hutton the piper's dead. My three-year
education ended. Bellows and bag
close round the belly for comfort; fingers dance
free on air, clean as a workman's whistle
timed to perfection. A crisp, dry wind,
cold off the moor's chest, sings like an angel thrush,
bursts from the earth bladder, reeding raw fifths,
under dancing stars on a drover's castle.

Spring reels on the river's ride, summer fruit
pudding of airs, moon's autumn jig, November
wind's lament and a heart-high hornpipe, all
stepped along the ranting hills. His music
beat the country heart green, tickling
tunes, like trout below the Thrum
and now (like chicken pox) he's passed it on,
infecting generations with his song.

Dave Medd

*The Northumbrian pipes are a quiet, domesticated, house-trained bagpipe. They
have been played in unbroken tradition in the north of England for at least 600
years. The bag is inflated by a bellows. A rant is a style of dance, also the tune
used for such.*

AUGUST

And now the year looks up,
scents north and starts to think
of slowly turning its head.
Now prophecies whisper themselves
of frost-beard where leaves
have slipped away,
of afternoons nodding to darkness.
The sun is two parts uncertainty
like a singer still just about
holding a tune. As often
as legs are slapped against midges,
so arms are rubbed unthinking,
shirts deemed adequate, just about,
till vacation blush
folds under equinoctial brown.

Time, perhaps, for a project
to set up dead straight
as the air starts to smell
of old attics. A jigsaw
of Judgement Day with as many pieces
as angels cleaving to a pin.
A walk that each morning
throws out another mile of leading-rope.
Losing the weight you ferried
across the longest days,
with a notion of seeing how thin you can get
so you hang loose and ruckled
round the self you once were,
so you slip through bars of shadow
without snagging a thread.
Or maybe just being
as still as a bird at refuge
while the days lose ballast
and bit by bit the sky unremembers
how to throw the stars easy
or pin them just right
so they cry the white of roses
all across a peaceable blue.

Michael W Thomas

Suffolk suffocating in high summer –
its cardboard cornfields warped by the sun
and pressed to the parched contours,
gasping for the rescue of harvest.
On their biscuit pasture
unbleating sheep clatter bleakly
over bleach-bladed, hoof-hard earth.

In the woods there's a smell of tobacco
and exotic *pot-pourri*.
Drought-drunk yellow leaves
drift dead-moth down to the path.
Boots kick crackling litter
like a Christmas frost-walk through leafdrifts
under sharp trees.

Out on the fields there's a different smell -
of harvested corn and earthdust.
The ostinato of combines
rumbles on well into the night
until star-strewn dampness stalls them.

Sunrise reveals a half-stubbled dawn.
                    *
Fifteen hundred miles to the east
there's a similar smell of harvest
but people in bed
hear the dull, dead din of artillery instead.
Dreams, lurching with every sudden loudness,
are fitful weavings of hope and dread,
the warp and weft of shrouds that
shape shadows of the dead.

Sunrise reveals a half-rubbled town.

And yet the harvest continues.
Past the tilted tanks the combines thunder,
beyond the mass graves in the woods
where boots disturb the reek of freshly dug soil,
and where guilt and shame, the one the other's twin,
crouch, hiding, in the sparse undergrowth,
reprising original sin.

Across uncertain acres the combines carve their way,
out-noising gunfire, playing their part
amongst the mash and the wort of human strife
where every dawn brings ferment of trouble -
an owl-eyed orphan, perhaps,
or a widowed wife
stumbling over a lifetime of rubble.
                    *
Harvest combinations:
a county scorched by the sun
and a country gored by the gun:
Suffolk after a heatwave; Ukraine after invasion.
Combining; combating.
Cornfields; minefields.
Reaping; raping.
Threshing; thrashing.
Gathering; smothering.
Milling; killing.
Stubble; rubble.

Rob Peel

THE INEVITABLE

The last sere leaf
on a Chestnut black branch
is blown away
by the Autumn wind,
and the book is closed.

Niels Hammer

Throwback

THE DIALECT OF WINTER

The row of poplars has its own
whispering arboreal *hygge*;
the guttural green of leeks survives
in the allotments on the edge of town.

Plot-holders speak to their spades,
discuss the canvas of the land, put
the finishing touches to the year.

Roofers and scaffolders barter
with their unique banter while
a wireless in the wind blares out
Good King Wenceslas looked out.

In an extension to the wine bar
there is winter in a tent with
the hissing patois of patio heaters.

Night is the kingdom of purple
and our blood a rich Tyrian hue.
A thin eloquence runs in our veins
and words catch fire in the dark.

Michael Henry

FROZEN

Our world slowed
as cold gnawed hard
through flinty earth.
Then feather kisses
swallowed up midwinter lead
made the garden into pillows
covered by a pristine spread

Mile on mile I tramped
day after day
along obliterated fields,
frost glittering every tree,
dog lolloping at my heels,
the heath a giant tablecloth
with cutwork hoofprints of deer

featherstitched by birds.

Whiteness seemed to bear us up,
spin prisms out of emptiness
like a great disco ball.
Dazzling light
lifted us from darkness, defeated night.
Stranded in icy brightness,
we drifted in and out the days.

Sun splintering snow
into rainbow fragments
must have sparked my search for colour.
Wheels, grids, compass-flowers
sprang beneath my cold-numbed hands
like fireworks
The elusive chromatic scale
beginning, ending bone

Sea a gleaming strip of steel
crowned marsh criss-crossed
by drift-choked dykes.
The ghost grey church shepherded
a crowd of dove-wing roofs.
Twilight receded.
In this bleached out world
every mid tone

lay heavy as stone.

We labour on like unmatched horses
harnessed together
pulling a sled through a silent landscape
which will never be dark,
never be warm.

Andria Cooke

Everybody here looks like the Duke of Edinburgh,
which isn't surprising. This is a lookalike convention
and I have just been awarded a 'commended'.

This might perhaps be seen as Western decadence.
Usually it's Ernest Hemingway but I don't possess
either his physique or puissant growth of beard.

Once, on the road back from Buchenwald to Weimar,
my East German friend told me I looked like a film-star.
"Der Michael sieht wie ein Schauspieler aus," he said.

And he said the same about his good-looking son,
who had come a cropper in the new united Germany.
I'm afraid, I, too, am one of life's cocker-uppers.

I'd like to write to my friend about my 'commended'.
But an iron shutter has sprung up between us
and I feel the hand of the cold war on my shoulder.

Michael Henry

HOW NOT TO SEE OURSELVES AS ITHERS SEE US
It wad frae mony a blunder free us,
Tae see oursels as ithers see us   Rabbie Burns

Be unrecognizable as the actor who, after his soap opera years
end with a well-publicised death, stands shivering with others,
a scarf pulled over his nose, as they unleash dogs that chase, yelp
while they all silently gaze through the mist at the sun slowly rising,
before – when his dog returns – he'll bare a face he's willing to show.

Ignore the Amazon algorithm that suggests more books
because they're similar to the one you've already ordered,
and Netflix which sends a text – *You must change your password*
because your account is being used on a Cumbrian TV
while you're watching a film at your in-laws' with popcorn and wine.
Gloss over Facebook's listing of friends you know are not friendly.
Make Skype play *Anarchy in the UK* to blast over what you say.

Be the one who waves at CCTV cameras, sidles into a side street,
returns slouch-shouldered in a different hat, so is never seen again

Bob Cooper

SELFIE

Put yourself up against a wall – brick or
acid-eaten stone will do – turn the phone

to selfie mode; try not to hunch or sken
and push away desire for all you should

have done. Avoid the rictus of those *en
route* to hell, look out of yourself to where

a dove is purring on the wire, to a house
where papers lie strewn and that loaf of

bread is whole but halfway sawn like a
woman in a circus act. Consider only facts

count to nought from another number
(not too high), say *cheese* or *testicles*

don't lag between thoughts, compose
yourself of all your many parts. Leave out

the sky, and when your mother/father
glares back, full of the silent rage of death

reflect that it's a likeness only, that nothing
is real, that you feel lighter than in years

that the world lies flat and cannot rise.

Graham Mort

My mother is naked. The veins in her see-through
skin are blue as ink. She stands in the daytime in the

daylight in the zinc bath where we scrape soap with
our fingernails. Lapped by a coal fire, my mother

sponges water ladled from the gas geyser. She doesn't
care who sees her. My mother throws a pad of cotton

on the fire, bright with the hurt of blood. My mother
goes to the doctor, a Polish man from the war with

steel spectacles. She keeps me with her, she leans
close to speak, hugs me on the bus because my

legs are cold, nibbles my ears like a mouse, snow
sliding from rooftops. I think it looks like pigeons

flying or washing laid out flat. My mother is in the rose
garden. Flowers grow from the soil, white and yellow

their petals scented, their thorns carnivorous. My
mother raises her arms and words fly back to my

father's mouth, bats hanging from the darkness he
broods in. My mother is naked. She slides through

oak curtains. She stands in eternity, raising her arms
as if they amaze her. Of all people she is herself.

She keeps me close. She doesn't care. Who sees her?

Graham Mort

Quietly she weeps again, like a small child,
very shyly, not wanting anyone to know,
but her body's slight trembles I can feel
as I awaken lying next to her, and so
I try comforting her, as her father might
have held her when she was just a young
girl after her dearest friend moved far away,
my face against her head, my arms slung
around her shoulders, holding her tight.

For two months, she's mourned the woman who
vanished so suddenly from our house, who'd once
charmed our friends and colleagues and knew
how to keep our guests bemused and speechless,
with her playful wit and flashing sapphire eyes.

The neurologists who examine her commend
her excellent progress, but she always sighs
at their words, privately wiping away fresh tears
by the time we reach the parking lot to leave,
because she now worries that the woman who
for so many years, wore her clothes, received
acclaim for her books, delivered her lectures,
is not the same one that I'll be driving home.

John Michael Sears

THE MARCHIONESS AT THE EDGE OF CLIFTON SUSPENSION BRIDGE
(Nicolette Fame 13/08/93)

It was supposed to be a day of no cause to mention again
so ordinary in August unmomentous, just cups of tea
a walk with my friend to clear the clutter from my head
a while pausing by the bridge, Clifton side,
where no sphinxes guard, the east rising a metre higher.
Catching sight of some sad woman leaning, unloading her keys
to some girls, leaning further and further over, she seemed balletic
as she slipped and slowly slid against the riffing of the path and chains.
I watched the way her hair ballooned 250 feet against the rushing wind
a parachute to break the fall but too slow the vanishing splash
and the woman gone
to tell me every day is a choice to stay
when leaving is as easy as a solo acrobatic display.

Kathryn Moores

After the accident you find there's no call
for a binman with one arm. Your fiancée
keeps the ring. You don't blame her.
You teach yourself to write with your other hand,
forming capital letters that never quite grow up.
And, never one for reading, you get a job in a library,
You learn the things that can't be done –
tying shoelaces, doing up buttons, cradling a child.
You buy a new car and a static on the coast,
where every weekend you have a seat at the club.

Stack the years in volumes, take the days,
file them away – 386, 793, 188.4
Because life's about knowing
what to discard, what to keep.
No more.

Liz McPherson

No Body

The skeleton alone remains
and my brain creates a person,
the way a hurried sketch
can conjure up a human,
or how we find a face
etched on a rock.

I scrape the soil back
with leaf trowel and toothpick,
scoop it into my bucket, tip it
on the spoil heap.
This used to be your guts,
your eyes and flesh.

I give you a name.

Tonnie Richmond

Cocoon

For Dr Caroline Wilkinson, Trimontium

Fulsome lover, a fraction your age,
she is holding your shattered skull.
Her fingers explore gaps,
dip into cavities, trenches,

trace shattered edges, touch the intimate,
inside ledges of antique reason.
She will detect your story's early dusk,
explore your husk, the bits you're missing.

Satisfied, in her moment,
you're safely dead,
she sets about making you ready,
shaping earth in your own image.

In the beginning,
she sticks pins in your debris,
builds your wax-flesh human,
around her significant scaffolding.

Feel her thumbs in your sockets,
pressing the ball race. Feel her
pinch cheek and lip,
deconstructing your smile.

Feel her tug at the root of your face.
She is twisting the lobes into place,
designing your grimace. Can you hear cartilage
creak, beneath her ministrations?

Your eyes are the colour of statistics,
Likewise your hair. What's left of it, black.
Cooling even now, your ardour,
she's in charge, at the back of your soul.

Dave Medd

GOLEM
(Prague, 1939)

For centuries I've lain here undisturbed,
this synagogue's hushed attic my bedchamber,
the life-spark in me stilled, sleep unperturbed.
Outside, folks chatter, kiss, curse. Few remember
how the Rabbis raised me up from fire and clay,
armoured in skin of thick Vltava mud,
stood sentry at the gates to bar the way
when fanatics stormed the city, screamed for blood.

Slanders have passed. A victim people thrive,
their guardian a fable or a phantom.
They think they do not need me to survive;
yet shadows gather once again to haunt them:
the crash of glass, the jack-boot at the door;
Chelmno, Treblinka, Terezin, Sobibor.

Andy Humphrey

MER-MAN

He skulks through the crack
between church doors,
wreathed in scents of seaweed,
of life wrapped in kelp and old rope.
The tolling bell
that on other days rings out
to warn of fog
or the onslaught of storms
falls silent at his coming.

He berths himself on the back pew
with a creak of blistered spars,
makes the sign of the cross
with yellow stubs of fingers.
At the elevated host
he bows his head, brushes
lank strands from eyes
damp with the memory
of comrades swallowed
in that swell of sea
beyond the high grey window.

He rises at the blessing,
tugs his ropes of clothes about him.
Shivers into the rain
as the organ pipes the final hymn.
In his wake:
a few stray green strands,
a patch of brine.
The ghost of an aroma
of tar and gutted fish.

Andy Humphrey

ALCUIN

I, Alcuin, scholar, poet, scribe,
Abbot of Marmoutier, teacher of Charlemagne
now face, like flowers of the garden, chill
winds of winter. All flesh fails.
Soon my soul, immortal, will be freed.

What lives on in this sad world are words,
of our Lord, mankind, and minds yet to be,
treasurehouse of our humanity,
shared in books, parchment, memory.

I rue only the love I must lose, the laughter
of friends that are no more.
                              And my homeland.

How well I recall that last journey
up the great river, wild geese twisting to flight,
noisily, from the banks; and beyond
the green wolds and woods of my birth.

By a village, children swim in the pools,
sunlight on wet skin, their shouts
a secret cry of pain.

Colin Speakman

PAIN PATHWAY

I've never told anyone this
but once, on the way back

from Skipton, I saw a wood pigeon
cleave its leg on a Range Rover

and fly away before
its nerves caught up.

I think about that bird
in the night, or when

the light seeps through,
when the pieces of me

that remain
start asking if I've noticed yet.

Laura Strickland

A bird takes flight.
You ask me why,
for there seems to be
no reason.

I think, and say:
To feather the air,
to river the height,
or *because it is skying season.*

Or: *Simply because they*
are there,
the blue of the sky
and the bird.

I love you, and
you ask me why;
there seems to be
no reason.

I cannot say
a sensible word
but think I see
by the blue in your eyes

the way you seem
to understand
the way that I'm
a bird.

James B. Nicola

I was the overcoat you wore for years –
trailing behind you, tripping you up.

I pinned badges under my collar
so only your heart knew their slogans

and when you held me close
to shut out the boys on the bus,

you read the letters I hid in my lining.
A bird built a nest in my sleeves,

threaded with the hair
of a girl you passed every morning,

and patched with pieces of your diary
you had cut and burned in the kitchen sink.

I started to smell
and people noticed how you never

took me off, even when it was time
to dance at the Friday disco.

My lining grew thinner
and I wish I'd warned you,

before the letters slipped out
and the bird flew into a window.

Laura Strickland

It's raining. I'm in the bus shelter, chilled and wet.
They're at the phone box. She's inside, talking.
He's outside, waiting.
    They swop places.
        I watch.
She comes over to me, holds out two fifty pence coins,
Have y' any change – these went straight through.
I swop them for coins in my hand. Hers are cold,
mine are warm. It's his mam, she says, real poorly.
I rummage in my pockets, find more silver.
Here's three more. I'll use a fiver for my fare.
We smile different smiles.
      She returns,
         tugs open the door,
gives him the coins, then waits. And was it tears
on her face or the same rain as on her thin coat,
her hair, her hands?
     I couldn't tell.
       The bus arrives,
I get on, pay, sit, see them stood on the pavement
while they talk, hug,
      walk into un-street-lit shadows
where they'll soon drape jackets over chair backs,
touch them occasionally to see if they're dry.

Bob Cooper

DECOMMISSIONED POLICE CAR

He drives a decommissioned police car.
There are holes in the dash where the radio used to be.
German shepherd teeth marks in the back of the head rests.
He likes to drive as if he's in the flying squad.
It's just that when he gets there there's no incident tape.
No incident at all. Only mum and dad or the car-park.
There's a confession scratched into the back of the passenger seat.
Some petty thief on the way to the station spelled out:
'I swear to God. It wasn't me'.

Steven Sivell

THE NICE MAN
i.m. Gurmail Singh, 1947 – 2010

House to house, he delivers papers on a sledge,
adds milk for snowbound pensioners, rings bells
and receives flashes of thanks in this uphill edge
of things where they only know his shopkeeper shell.
He brings news of cup ties and celebrity dates –
this small lion who works seven cheerful days,
loves Leeds United, finds he's constantly amazed
at how faith grows and grandchildren graduate.

Each time I drive to town, I see those onion domes –
yellow as sunflowers – that crest his spiritual home,
the Gurdwara, 'doorway to God', place of welcome
for those late, long weddings when we cover our hair,
sit painfully cross-legged, share food and prayer.

Club hammer, police tape. Cigarettes. Chewing gum.

Adam Strickson

Just Behind the Morning

WITNESSING
"Today I have no god but landscape, and no expectation of death but extinction."
John le Carré

A knock
mid-morning Saturday –
a parcel, offers to
replace our windows, cut down trees?
"After two years
we've started calling round again"
(lockdown spared us that, at least).
Their leaflet promises
"The joy of life forever."
You had just read
le Carré's memoir
and quoted it to them;
I wonder what they made of it.
I laughed; I think le Carré
would have been amused.

Heather Deckner

Sometimes, when you need help returning to
your body, which has strayed so far from you,
a frozen river can help.

A burning cold can cauterise the galaxy of
wounds etched on your flimsy heart.
Can call the body back.

Break thin ice and wade. The glacial river-pull will
tug flesh & bone, will unknot ankles, will grasp the
curve of your hips, pinch your nipples, clutch your
ribcage so tight you are lung-squeezed to take a
breath so deep your wandering body returns.

Feel the tiny minnow's quiet mouths feed from
the soft skin of your feet. Listen. You can hear
your new sub-aquatic blood-coursing rhythms.
They sound like hope. Like rivers.

Emily Zobel Marshall

6.30 drinkers, pints already pulled.
In the dimmed, yellow light,
watching, fascinated …

Off to the side,
with my back against the wall,
I'm suddenly thinking of Whitman,
of Whitman waiting for his love
in *A Glimpse*.

But this isn't that.
There's no waiting here.
There's no pooling of the potential for love,
only the sticky stains of poorly wiped tables.

With eyes in pints,
gathered round the flashing 'deal or no deal'
of a fruit machine, they have nothing to say,
except that they've all missed breakfast.

No, this is waiting of a different kind,
and over the curved lipped rim,
I watch the slow, slipping drift of it.

The leather-skinned face
with a black spot,
slowly aging,
standing on ceremony
and looking about,
is gazing off into it.

The man with a hooked nose,
with his old man's brown coat,
stained around the collar,
is doing the same,
setting his pint down precisely.

The young blue tracksuit,
his white Tesco bag filled with tinnies,
is here for the long haul,
is acquiring the same vacant stare.
There's a break in the routine.

A release for a smoke!
I'm watching the slow,
slipping drift of it.

They all seem to know.
They all share the same unspoken knowledge
that they're all alcoholics,
drifting silently through
the days of weekly years,
gazing along the slow,
drifting rhythm of it.

Seeing it that much clearer, perhaps.

Steven Lightfoot

It was a Tuesday evening, the television repeated itself, and I was
bored or peckish. You suggested a walk but we never did. I know,
I thought, I'll eat the world, and began with a lick of the Adriatic.
The salt on my tongue got me going, so I bit into Africa, tasting dusty
roads, hospitals and mineral deposits, swallowing noisy goats
and children. Russia next, so cold and tough in parts, and chewy
with all that forest. Then America, fat humans bursting with sugar
and cheese. England was a little starchy. France, Italy and Spain
were best, the wine and cheese alongside cries of people
imploring Mary to help them, but that was not my name and I
wasn't wearing blue. On I went, devouring rain forests,
shopping malls, Amazon warehouses, owls, dogs, birds,
kangaroos, swimming pools, cars, drug dens, cruise ships,
amusement arcades, petrol stations, factories, the lot. I began to feel
bloated and sick, but by now was on a roll and kept eating,
fuelled by something boundless, and when it was done,
merciless belching overcame me. There was blood on my chin.
I looked at the moon and the sun, but you glared. 'Don't you dare,'
you said, snarling. 'The stars stay where they are. Otherwise,
we'll be in darkness, and you know what happened last time.'
The International Space Station whizzed about like a delirious
metal bee. I would have eaten that, but by that time I was much too full.

Miles Salter

He tears round the kitchen on all-fours
my chameleon eyes watch from table's vantage
over a cooling meal. I launch like a flicking tongue
as his explorer's fingers approach the cat's food
as he flings open cupboards, treasure's gleam
reflected in his face, as he begins the ascent
scaling the dishwasher's heights.

He hauls himself up with the table leg
balance improving. His eyes smile
with glee as he reaches his latest zenith
leans back to check for my attention.
I lurch to place a hand behind him
stroke that head with hint of down
the shape of his skull unmasked.

A buffet spread of plastic toys is laid out
every morsel sucked, chewed and discarded
a building-block train, funnel removed
a set of eight stacking cups, only seven in sight
and a rubber menagerie in primary colours
collected wild beasts of assorted habitat
their bodies unbreakable on the tiled floor.

David Thompson

HOW YOU ROSE
For Rose

When you swim
you send snakes of Spring sunlight
slithering across pitch waters
from bank to bank

Bewitched by your circling stroke
I wonder at your survival
how you rose cleanly
from the suck of treacherous currents
over and over again

While Dad and I knew all the timings
memorised the names of drugs
it was you who learnt
to move your body forwards

I see the tight muscles on your back
the surprise of slick long hair
your healing was determined
by your own stroke

I slide into the river
feel the punch of Winter lingering
tail you as you move
through uncertain, dappled rays
your strong bare feet kicking
great kaleidoscopic
arcs of spray
skyward

Emily Zobel Marshall

PEANUT

Our daughter was delicious as a toddler.
We called her Peanut, baby Pea for short.

There was an awkward moment in Madrid:
border control checked her name to prove

she was ours. Both of us looked guilty
hoping she'd react to her given name.

Then the news, full of atrocity – child abuse
and murder. Baby P's parents in court accused.

And I raged. They'd ruined it. Baby Pea died
on our tongues as the news unravelled.

I went to church, prayed for understanding
caught hold of the vicar: how did this happen?

Why did that little boy suffer so much pain?
Couldn't God have swapped him with mine?

I'm sorry, she said, wearily
you know it doesn't work like that.

Verity Baldry

No One Tells You
(after Rita Ann Higgins)

what it's like

to hear a man call your child a *little twat* in the Co op
to be told your two year old doesn't *join in* at nursery
to be called out of work for a torn coat
to have your child expelled for meltdowns
to have endless appointments cancelled by professionals
to be told off when you miss one
to have scripts for medication you can't pronounce
to be asked why your child is obsessed with washing machines
to have the police called for paint daubs on a neighbour's wall
to be punched so hard in the arm your hand slips on the gearstick
to have a whole hanging basket dropped on your head
to have your house trashed at 2am

to be the one thing standing between home and a secure unit.

Laura Strickland

MISCARRIAGE

Agony loads the air with chrysanthemums.
Odours, like a dark star, leach their pollen
into my bloodstream. Coal-black snowflakes etch
design that doubled you, needle under brain rind,
picking synapses till they jangled.

Pain was your remit, hailing a star's existence.
Years, we believed it impossible. Now, the forensic,
evident, tell-tale, ghost-stained mocked our sheets.
Can that be how it works? Each of us loitering
out in chaos, waiting on blueprints of glory?

Well. We were all fingers and thumbs, and yet,
your wanderer came calling, took up residence.
Had we guessed, we'd have sheltered the spark from catastrophe;
sat by the fire, hand-join cups around
your tiny glittering. Oh, we'd have breathed on you

All the delight we could muster! So there you are,
intake of sudden breath, one butterfly word,
or a moth, whose wing beats bring down tyrants. And when
we turn on shadow, unseen hand on the shoulder,
silent rumour of night stock, in empty gardens,

this remains, your twenty-four year echo.
Once, we must have loved enough,
      attracting a star.

Dave Medd

Miranda said *the best things in life are free,*
stole sweets from the corner shop.

Granddad wore his Sunday best to the beach,
swore long johns kept the heat out.

Rob cracked the best Best Man jokes,
said he was fine. He wasn't.

Hubbie loves beans on toast and cheese sarnie;
best dinners after a holiday.

Mum's best china went to the charity shop
with the 137 teddies she couldn't remember.

The birthday card from my six year old I kept,
you're the beast Mum, still the best words ever.

Sandra Noel

REVIEWS

Imperfect Beginnings by Viv Fogel
Fly on the Wall Press
ISBN 978 1 913211 98 1   £9.99

Adrienne Rich, in reviewing Elizabeth Bishop's *The Complete Poems*,
for *The Boston Review* in 1983, highlighted Bishop's perspective as an
outsider and emphasised how the outsider's eye enables her

'to perceive other kinds of outsiders and to identify, or try to
identify, with them.'

In the prologue to this moving and compelling collection, Fogel writes:

'I will never quite belong – I will always be other – an outsider.'

The collection is appropriately titled as, like Bishop, Fogel's family was
disrupted, adopted before she was a year old by two Holocaust survivors,
her adoptive mother being bi-polar, seeking to construct a sense of where
she might have come from, meeting her birth mother in a poignant poem.

Issues of belonging, dislocation and sundering pervade the poems which
search for personal and societal connection – 're-membering,' as Fogel
puts it, the putting back of what has been abruptly cut off. The opening
poem, "Exiled", with its short gasps of lines and broken, open verse says
it all:

'I was alone
no roots
no ground.'

As Rich suggested for Bishop, this perspective does give Fogel empathy
for outsiders, notably the asylum seekers that currently dominate the
British news. Those like Ahmad who see their lives as

'a stagnant pool where nothing lives or moves.'

Or the waterlogged man who stumbles from a dinghy into the arms of a
volunteer,

'for a moment he is in the arms of his mother'

("Ahmad's Pool") and, indeed, such comfort is what these fiercely
honest and unsentimental poems may well offer in their human empathy.

The Holocaust and the Nazis are a thread. Fogel, who was born in 1948,
had no first-hand knowledge but her perspectives are no less valid –

'we improvise
singing songs we've never heard.'

("Still Point"). It might be thought that little new could be written about
the massacre of six hundred people by Waffen-SS soldiers at Oradour-Sur

– Glane in 1944, but Fogel's eponymous poem is elevated by the focus on detail, by her eye for,

'resin comb, button, the peeling paint of a toy truck
a child's scuffed shoe'

– red in the ash grey ruins. Her poems, similarly, glow in a monochrome world.

It is almost as if Fogel has felt compelled to visit these dark places, to seek some understanding and to bear witness despite their being in the past. She sees the typical iconography of the death camps and recognises

'many will roll their eyes *move on*
so I do not write about the Holocaust
I was not there   I was not there'

("On Not Writing the Holocaust"). Yet, of course, she was there as all who hope that such things will never be forgotten need to be there. To know and not to speak, is not to know and Fogel does seek to know and speak however painful memories are. She delves deeply into the her past – directly and indirectly – but is never trapped by it, indeed her poetry is liberated by it and her concerns for the dispossessed of today seem firmly rooted in such transcendence.

Fogel is a confident poet in handling her material and has a no-nonsense approach to expressing herself –

'I don't want clever
I want simple and true
words that take me to the raw.'

("How It Is"). She is not constrained by the 'safety of lines,' preferring the

'blank page, to dive
and spiral bird free in a cloudless sky'
("Notebooks").

If she dives, she comes up smiling – her work as a psychotherapist helpful in enabling her to navigate the personal and historical challenges – and there is a strong human spirit of optimism here, an honest and beneficial perspective gained –

'the leaving and the return
as the tide comes and goes
the breathing in   the breathing out'

("What Remains (A Conversation)"). This is a good collection, uplifting and accessible in its hope and essential "grounded-ness", in its recognition that, no matter what, the sun also rises and in this we can seek our consolations.

Patrick Lodge

Flamingo by Kathryn Bevis
Seren
ISBN 9781781726938, pp35 £6.00

From the off, Bevis' debut pamphlet takes no prisoners. 'Fuck that. I want to take up room' declares "Wonder Woman," questioning her "status as a '70s Symbol of Female Empowerment". Each of the poems in this slim volume expands to fill more than the space often allocated to the female of the species, whether they be real women, such as Bevis', 'Nan-Nan', 'casting herself off' in a care home; the disturbingly nested "Matryoshka," whose wooden core is both

> 'the hatchling
> and the egg,'

or the life model, being shown the ropes by her Union Representative, and advised:

> 'Try to get a kip in, if you can.'

We also meet a bunch of teddy bears, modelling coercive controlling behaviour, and a deftly-depicted "Delinquent." Bevis draws on irony, surrealism and close observation of the material world to describe the alienation we can feel from our fallible bodies. Several of the poems focus on serious bodily ills (her own and others'); in "My body tells me that she's filing for divorce," "In this poem, your routine bloods have come back normal" as well as the title poem, Bevis tries on – like sample garments – the forms of separation that mortality has in store for people living with cancer. There's humour and courage in the realisation that 'We both know one day she'll eat me.' ("My Cancer as a Ring-Tailed Lemur"). Bevis faces up to the inevitability of death by insisting on living as vibrantly as possible.

Meanwhile, the urgency of the present moment is captured again and again: here's a poet who can delight in a gannet's beak 'piercing the linen of mist' and the way grey wagtails

> 'translate water
> to sunlight, sunlight to water.'

This is a collection that wakes you up, pushes you adrift from your comfort zone – and then sends you a life buoy, to bring you to the shore.

Hannah Stone

The Way Taken: A Chinese Expedition by Dave Wynne-Jones
Delfryn Publications
ISBN 978-1-9163674-1-8   £5.00

In his preface Dave Wynne-Jones says, 'On my first expedition to China, I took a translation of *The Selected Poems of Li Po* by David Hinton and Ursula le Guin's *Tao te Ching*. It was not an easy trip but my reading helped me come to terms with events in the poems that I wrote during that time. Years later ... I rediscovered these poems and revised and added to them.'

Li-Po's influence can be seen throughout this collection. It conveys the impact of Chinese culture on a western sensibility, in poetry that draws on the Chinese classical tradition.

The shorter poems have a proverbial quality, as in "Waymaking":

'For every way we
follow there are other ways
we could have taken.'

Longer poems use natural detail to allude to an emotion or event, as in the opening of "On Chola Mountain":

'Where summer yak pastures grow sparse,
deep blue of alpine gentians gives way
to a scattering of eggshell blue and white'...

The beauty of the poet's companion (lover?) is only touched on in the last line.

This approach may bewilder a western reader. "Wu-wei" and "Travelling Between the Passes" appear full of scattered images, but these are being used to convey deeper meanings. Traditional Chinese symbols also accompany some poems. These add to the mood of the poem, so it is helpful to refer to the glossary.

Wynne-Jones calls his poems 'a travelogue'. While they give glimpses of Tibet, extreme weather and local hostility, details remain vague. As a westerner I found this lack of narrative disappointing, and the hints of a broken relationship frustrating. "To Send Far Away" led me to expect more on this theme, but classical Chinese poetry never bares its soul.

To fully appreciate this collection, then, the reader needs to appreciate the tradition within which it is written. It is an interesting read, however, without this knowledge.

Pauline Kirk

Bodies and other haunted houses by S L Grange
Seren
ISBN 9781781726815 pp 34 £5.00

S L Grange's pamphlet, which won the Poetry Wales Pamphlet prize, is written from and for the LGBTQIA+ community, and themes of gender identity, in the present and through history, are at the angry beating heart of this collection. Currently engaged in PhD research into how to 'do' Queer history, Grange summons demonised daemons and role models from the past, notably Mary Frith, (a London cross-dressing performer and criminal active in the sixteenth and seventeenth centuries), and Amina of Zazzau, a noted African warrior of the same period. We meet witches (seeded in an account of the Pendle witch trials of 1612). They also reveal personal experiences of evolving and discriminated selfhood, through memorable epiphanies. Reading the poems in the capital on the day of a recent coronation, I was especially taken by the re-working of the final verse of Cecil Spring-Rice's well-known patriotic hymn:

'I vow to thee my cunt
All earthly things above
Entire and whole and perfect
The service of my love.'

In Grange's poems, loyalty to the contested ground of the queer body is hard-earned, through journeys of discovery and transformation. We learn that 'Desire is a ghost', and

'What our bodies love is liberty
from each other's progress

What our bodies love is liberty
from the same blasted wasteland.'
("This shit is killing you…").

There are adventures in form, too, with 'After Sappho' presenting as a multi-layered part found, part ekphrastic poem, 'inspired by Anne Carson's translations of poetry fragments' but also 'a response to degraded VHS archive footage of Split Britches/Bloolips 1990 collaborative performance *Belle Reprieve*.' (I did notice that the explanatory note was almost as long as the poem itself.)

Yes, maybe 'All of this has been written before' ("Queer Times"), but every generation brings its new scribes and voices. S L Grange's is surely one to be read, listened to, and transmitted, now no longer just through 'lipstick on powder-room mirrors' and 'squatted over rare snowfalls' writing their names 'in pure piss,' but on the pages of this evocative and haunting collection.

Hannah Stone

Something the Colour of Pines on Fire by **Vahid Davar**
Matecznik Press
ISBN 978-1-9160847-1-1 £5.00

This short pamphlet must serve as only an introduction to the poetry of
Vahid Davar, an Iranian refugee who came to Britain in 2013. The
collection largely consists of extracts from two major collections in Persian
and published, *in absentia*, in 2018/19. The pamphlet, self-translated by
the poet whose facility in English is exceptional, contains, as he writes, 'all
my semi-self-translated exodus poems.' It is a remarkable collection in its
scope, imaginative power, verbal dexterity and strong emotional heft – it
should be required reading for all Home Secretaries.

Davar has written that 'he fled from a burning homeland, scorched and
almost smothered' and, unsurprisingly, the experience suffuses all the
poems here, not least the three sections from the superb "Nassim's
Testament" sequence. This is a *tour-de-force* of inspired creativity that
seamlessly blends the asylum-seekers' experiences with religious,
historical, literary and other cultural references without ever losing the
polemical punch. Davar has described the sequence as a kind of 'wake'
and, as such, it 'laments, tells tales, cracks jokes, performs dances and
experiments with various modes of poetic expression.'

Davar saw his escape to the UK as an opportunity to 're-visualise'
himself and adopts a subtle *alter ego* and a companion witness, Nassim, a
non-gendered resurrection of his close friend, the poet Nassimi who had
killed himself several years before Davar's arrival in the UK. Here are two
suffering voices as one – 'I, who am both Nassim and Vahid' ("The Bright
Salt") – who join in 'a combined act of creation.'

Davar describes his main technique in exploring his journey as
'ventriloquising' – in effect, Vahid and Nassim project other voices –
Davar worked, in Liverpool, as an interpreter for other refugees – which
allows the poet to adopt a protean self and roam wild and free across time
and cultures. In a sense the poet ceases to exist: he has noted that crossing
continents in an Ark-like shipping container – like Jonah in the whale, the
story that prompts Davar's cover art – a person becomes immaterial, can
drift like a spirit through anything – they become

> 'ghosts
> who fled at midnight in a shipping container'

("The Bright Salt"). The poetry magically and skilfully reflects this as
Vahid and Nassim are 'suspended in mid-air' hanging between Shiraz and
Liverpool unable to root anywhere but using that disassociation to make
seamless transitions between Iran and the UK, history and the present, real
and imagined.

Davar – himself an artist – often makes several references to artworks
and has termed his approach ekphrastic but it seems less that the poems

respond to particular paintings than that Vahid and Nassim inhabit them – notably Rembrandt's "The Sacrifice of Isaac" and Breughel's "The Fall of the Rebel Angels," the latter providing a powerful emotional weight to the protagonists' encounters with the whimsical god UKBA (the UK Border Agency) who presides over the 'court on the seashore' which greets refugees, identifying 'good' refugees and 'bad' refugees:

'And the English saw
that strange shower…' and like Iranian fishermen,

'separate the salmon
from the sole and the starfish.'
("The Sole and the Salmon").

Davar writes in translation with a seductive lyricism and effortless blending of various mythologies and narratives. Section 8, "The Tale Nassim told Nassim, or Maryam Related to Vahid" interweaves Halloween, the late Queen Elizabeth and two Iranian fairy tales – which, as Dr Yass Alizadeh has written, were often used as a powerful and urgent response to post-revolutionary Iranian reality and a subversive challenge to the power structure. Throughout Davar utilises an almost Biblical phraseology – 'a strongly felt presence' as he once wrote – which elevates his journey into an epic. Davar sees the Bible as a great book of exile – but of relation not separation and, indeed, such epics were written in antiquity precisely to promulgate a people's legitimacy, to root them in a collective meaning. This sense of 'unbelonging', of being between two worlds, even after 'taking an oath in the name of the old woman' and singing 'God Bless the Nana,' pervades the collection. The outstanding "Pastoral 1", with its repeated request to 'Imagine,' referencing John Lennon's plea for peace and togetherness from Davar's new home of Liverpool, ends on the resonant and close to perfect image of un-rootedness and loss;

'Imagine
the Smithdown cemetery held your blood relatives.'

The collection ends with "From Sea to Dawn" – a commissioned poem inspired by, and displayed with, a video artwork of the same title by an Iranian collective which intervenes in and subverts common media imagery of migrants. The poem is a fitting close in its optimistic yet grounded realism with its evocations, 'O King of Righteousness' to 'Wear a life jacket, wear a life jacket' and 'O Spirit' to

'be a living foil blanket sheeted around us in the cold…
Say 'let there be rotating police beacons'
And there will be light.'

A subtle end to this masterful pamphlet. There are currently no plans to publish a translation of the full sequences which form the backbone of this work – though the text of "Nassim's Testament", with its Persian original, is included in the British Museum exhibit *Atlas of the World* (2022). Such a collection would be a major edition to contemporary poetry and an important contribution to any debate about policy on asylum-seekers.

Patrick Lodge

Surrender by Cathy Grindrod
Five Leaves
ISBN: 978-1-910170-95-3 pp 112

Grindrod has an enviable track record; not only has she several poetry publications under her belt, but she is a playwright and composer, having been nominated for a BBC Composer of the Year Award. This collection marks her return to poetry after a twelve-year absence. It is a potted personal history, retold through a variety of voices – daughter, mother, partner, writer, and not forgetting "Portrait of Myself as Angel."

The opening and closing poems end on, 'open your mouth and' – she's telling us, she's telling us. The second poem, "First", tells us this is her life and her work:

> 'I reached out for a hand to hold
> and finding my own
> took it.'

"What I love About Donkeys" has a pleasing – and fitting – simplicity. A series of couplets, including lines like:

> 'that their legs somehow support their weight...

> that they knew Jesus
> that their purpose is steadfast

> that we happen around them
> that they have time, time, time'

Section two – a series of "days" as mileposts – with excellent titles like "The Woman Who Thinks the Stapler Is Hers" or "The Man Who Books a Meeting With Himself", captures the horror of office life and politics, with daily 'messages of motivation' and 'uniquely numbered set of drawers, uniquely numbered frame' for "An image of your choice."

"Despite School" starts with the 'whatever' of partially learned History – Tudors, Iron Age, etc. – before moving nicely and affectingly into personal histories from around the place she grew up:

> '...the hospital Grandad still called
> The Workhouse, shuddering.'

This is a gentle collection, with breathing spaces: many of the pages are blank, as the start and finish of each of the nine sections is marked by a title page and a blank.

Nick Allen

Journey Into Space by Seán Street
Shoestring Press
ISBN 9-781912 524877   pp53 £10.00

Seán Street's tenth collection resists the common trend to focus entire collections on a single theme. The collection is, however, ventilated by structuring into sets of poems – clusters of 4, 6, 9 at a time –which hang together with an inner coherence. Among these, the title poem (from the section "Littoral") touches on a matter of deep interest to the sound-recordist turned poet: the very nature of sound, and how the airwaves can both bring together and separate disparate people. The emotional impact of musical sounds is also featured:

'… Music is more than its sound' he tells us ("At the Window"),

and in "Islandness" Street explains:

'how deep a music's blade
can cut, how a grace note's ornament
sung as the roof's storm beat that night, cracked
open then broke the listening heart.'

"Handwritten" shows how the word on the page can be less vivid than the auditory communication; indeed, it is the

'sounds we made [that] still make us,
the grain of particulars.'

This focus on the power of sound and silence to evoke and transmit meaning recalls R S Thomas' poem "Kneeling" –

'… the air a staircase
For silence …. Prompt me, God;
But not yet. When I speak,
Though it be you who speak
Through me, something is lost.
The meaning is in the waiting.'

Street is also self-conscious about the craft of the poet:

'Now I loosen stacked words from the page's lumber,
Try to shape a poem as tangible as you.'
("Apple wood").

Another feature that springs out from the page is Street's sensitivity to the liminal – both temporal and physical. In poems reminiscent of his earlier collection *The Sound Recordist*, Street captures the moments between day and night (a period I know he feels has especial auditory qualities); "On the Air," "Slant," and "Evening" are especially vivid examples of this. The potential of estuaries to move, transform and create is evoked in the "Rivering" section, whose opening poem, "Shoreline," reminds us that, in an ephemeral world,

'Each breaker [is]a line and each rock that ends
It a rhyme, every tide a new poem.'

Published when the poet was in his seventies, this is in many ways a retrospective collection, and several of the poems refer directly to cultural and global events from the poet's youth and childhood which may not always be intelligible to younger readers. Here, the copious endnotes provide context for historical excavations, as well as for the many ekphrastic poems; this can smack a little too much of the academic, wanting to provide references in case challenged. Perhaps he is most at ease, most shaped as a poet, when mulling over his engagement with sensory stimuli.

Hannah Stone

***Angola, America* by Sammy Weaver**
Seren
ISBN: 978-1-78172-700-3 pp 33

(Winner of the Mslexia Poetry Pamphlet Competition 2021)

"Angola" is the Louisiana State Penitentiary, the largest maximum-security prison in the US. It is also the name of the plantation that stood on this site before it became home to the penitentiary and a farm. Angola sits in a tremendous oxbow of the Mississippi, as far downstream from Natchez as it is upstream from Baton Rouge:

'The great flat flooded
Flooding
floodable lands of cotton, slavery and the blues.'

Weaver, a woman living on a narrow boat in West Yorkshire, struck up a correspondence friendship with an inmate on death row. This stunning collection, electric with fury, injustice, inhumanity and questions about race, details Weaver's reflections on and response to that correspondence.

All the titles are hemmed-in, contained, manacled, they are *imprisoned* in brackets.

From "[correspondence : another year]"

'… & the line ignites into song as you sing to me

happy birthday & because birth is death in reverse
    I imagine blowing a candle out backwards, sucking

the orange talons into the prison of my lungs
    the wax congealing up the wick, the match lying

down in its box, the rush of our bodies diminishing
    inside the bodies of our mothers'

Driven by quotations from Angela Davis and Claudia Rankine, we are not just here as witness to the degradation, the violence, the everyday brutal racism of the American penal – and judicial – system, we are being challenged to take sides: to acknowledge that this is not the way a civilized society treats people, and certainly not the way to eradicate criminality:

'But prisons do not disappear problems, they disappear human beings'
("Davis.")

Whether through the prism of the horrific decision to replace guards with half-breed wolf/dogs, or through the contemplation of which tree gave its wood to be the electric chair ("Gruesome Gertie"), we are offered little respite. The language, the choice of words and how they are placed, is sharp; they are meant to draw blood. The control is admirable. We are invited to read and re-read as the double-meanings, the asides and the slants reveal themselves. It is sparse and it is beautiful. And it is terrible.

There are odes to the 'shiv', to 'handcuffs', and of course 'escapism' – a lower key meditation on the things that are small enough to pass between the bars: 'motes,' 'moonlight,' 'pipistrelles,' and 'quarks.'

Someone is learning First Aid, some inmates are competing in the annual Angola rodeo –

'to be gored is both honour & disgrace…
until finally, they are broken-boned & returned to their cages'

and there is a prison spiritual featuring Dr John, Lil' Boosie and Leadbelly.

In the final poem "[correspondence : videogram]" her correspondent is shown repeatedly replaying the 30 second clip of a sunset she sent him:

'Because there is nothing

more lonely than a window,
except the drawing of a window

on a windowless wall. You lie back,
letting this relic of sunset fill your cell.'

I have re-read this several times, looking for the redemption, there is none.

'Better then to leave
the beads of sweet sweat uncorrected.'
(From "[state soap]")

It is an exhilarating and exacting collection of poems, which illustrates why poetry remains at the forefront of ferocious expose and protest.

Nick Allen

The Doll's Hospital by Jenny Robb
Yaffle
ISBN 9781913 122294   pp 64   £10.00

A new release from the entrepreneurial local Yaffle Press, Jenny Robb's debut collection *The Doll's Hospital* makes an immediate impact. The title's echo of Ibsen's play brought to mind images of constraint, and emancipation, with Nora in *The Doll's House* breaking out of the confines of bourgeois expectations and domesticity; Robb's metaphorical dolls are confined by different experiences, and more in need of repair, whether from painfully captured family trauma, the experience of being a 'boomer' woman, or health challenges. "Rosebud" seems to project the disintegration of family life "The day Dad disappeared."

Robb adopts an autobiographical tone for the majority of the poems, and her first person narrator navigates through memories of an absent would-be poet father, who struggled with parenthood and the expectations placed on men, through the choppy waters of relationships and mothering, to a measure of joyful acceptance. The collection is bookended with references to happier experiences, be it adolescent explorations of sex or the more mature intimacy of

'… Making up
with sex seasoned by years of practice.'

It is here Robb finds her "Happy place," and there is more than one 'Zipless fuck' along the way to add leaven. Unlike Nora, Robb is able to find release without tragedy.

But before that we have the agonised realisation that

'Your dad's sensitive, pushed too soon, too far by ambitious parents.'

In a chilling re-telling of A. A. Milne, we learn of his suicide attempts and incarceration in mental asylums. Ever the survivor, Robb chooses not to follow suit, and

'Chemicals, therapy, lover and friends
coax me back from the edge.'

A handful of the poems replace this focus on the personal emotional journey with reflections on more external events, with allusions to the political protests of Thatcherite Britain. Here is a strong new voice, that many women will empathise with.

Hannah Stone

INDEX OF AUTHORS

Adam Strickson 91
Andria Cooke 72
Andy Humphrey 83, 84
Bill Fitzsimons 8
Bob Cooper....................74, 89
Chris Scriven 7
Clifford Liles 20
Colin Speakman 85
D M Street 58
Dave Medd 65, 82, 102
David Danbury 19
David McVey 26
David Thompson 98
Denise McSheehy..................60
Edward Alport 64
Emily Zobel Marshall......94, 99
George Jowett........................10
Graham Mort.................75, 76
Greg McGee 1
Hannah Stone 3, 4, 106, 108,
    112, 115
Harry Slater 6
Heather Deckner....................93
Jaimes Lewis Moran..............36
James B. Nicola 87
Jane Ayrie..............................44
Jane Sharp.............................50
Jaspreet Mander....................32
Jeff Phelps 56
John Michael Sears...............77

Joseph Estevez......................53
Kathryn Moores....................78
Knotbrook Taylor 21, 39
Laura Strickland 86, 88, 101
Lauren K. Nixon.............52, 57
Liz McPherson......................79
Mark Pearce..........................42
Michael Henry 71, 73
Michael Newman...................51
Michael Penny 63
Michael W Thomas 23, 66
Miles Salter...........................97
Nick Allen 111, 113
Niels Hammer........................69
Owen O'Sullivan 12
Patrick Lodge..............104, 109
Paul Brownsey.......................13
Paula Jennings 41
Pauline Kirk..........................107
Philip Burton 54
Ray Malone 55
Rob Peel................................67
Sandra Noel 103
Simon Tindale 40
Steven Lightfoot 95
Steven Sivell...............9, 31, 90
Sue Moules 22
Tonnie Richmond 80
Verity Baldry 100
Wilf Deckner 24

Other anthologies and collections available from Stairwell Books

The Estuary and the Sea	Jennifer Keevill
In | Between	Angela Arnold
Quiet Flows the Hull	Clint Wastling
Lunch on a Green Ledge	Stella Davis
there is an england	Harry Gallagher
Iconic Tattoo	Richard Harries
Fatherhood	CS Fuqua
Herdsmenization	Ngozi Olivia Osuoha
On the Other Side of the Beach, Light	Daniel Skyle
Words from a Distance	Ed. Amina Alyal, Judi Sissons
Fractured	Shannon O'Neill
Unknown	Anna Rose James, Elizabeth Chadwick Pywell
When We Wake We Think We're Whalers from Eden	Bob Beagrie
Awakening	Richard Harries
A Stray Dog, Following	Greg Quiery
Blue Saxophone	Rosemary Palmeira
Steel Tipped Snowflakes 1	Izzy Rhiannon Jones, Becca Miles, Laura Voivodeship
Where the Hares Are	John Gilham
The Glass King	Gary Allen
A Thing of Beauty Is a Joy Forever	Don Walls
Gooseberries	Val Horner
Poetry for the Newly Single 40 Something	Maria Stephenson
Northern Lights	Harry Gallagher
Nothing Is Meant to be Broken	Mark Connors
Heading for the Hills	Gillian Byrom-Smith
More Exhibitionism	Ed. Glen Taylor
The Beggars of York	Don Walls
Lodestone	Hannah Stone
Unsettled Accounts	Tony Lucas
Learning to Breathe	John Gilham
New Crops from Old Fields	Ed. Oz Hardwick
The Ordinariness of Parrots	Amina Alyal
Homeless	Ed. Ross Raisin
49	Paul Lingaard
Sometimes I Fly	Tim Goldthorpe
Somewhere Else	Don Walls
Still Life with Wine and Cheese	Ed. Rose Drew, Alan Gillott
York in Poetry Artwork and Photographs	Ed. John Coopey, Sally Guthrie

For further information please contact rose@stairwellbooks.com

www.stairwellbooks.co.uk
@stairwellbooks